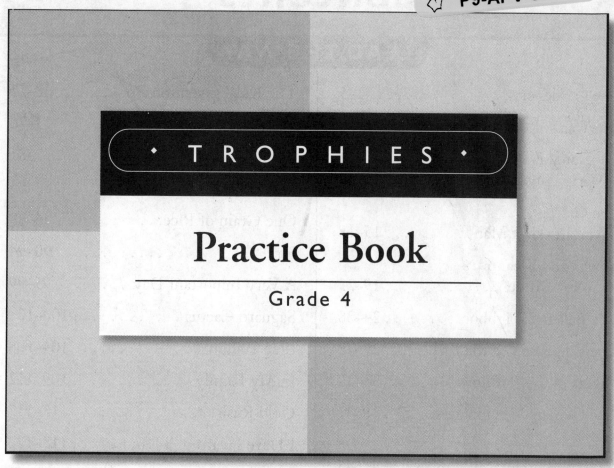

· TROPHIES ·

Practice Book

Grade 4

Harcourt

Orlando   Boston   Dallas   Chicago   San Diego

Visit *The Learning Site!*
www.harcourtschool.com

Printed in the United States of America

ISBN 0-15-323522-5

15 16 17 18 054 10 09 08 07 06

Contents

LEAD THE WAY

Name _____

▶ **Use the Vocabulary Words to complete the sentences in the letter. Some words will be used twice.**

anxious	recognizing	adore	vacant	sprucing	retire

Dear Uncle Jim,

I'm glad to be back home with Mama, Papa, and Grandma, but at

the same time, I miss you. I really did **(1)** _____

living in the city and making the **(2)** _____

rooftop into a flower garden paradise.

Since I've been home, I've been busy **(3)** _____ up

my room. I did not **(4)** _____ as a gardener, either!

There is a **(5)** _____ lot outside my window where I

have planted all kinds of colorful flowers. I am **(6)** _____

to send you a picture as soon as the flowers are in full bloom.

I'm growing even faster than the flowers. **(7)** _____ me will

be a challenge for you next time I visit.

I know you still must be working hard in the bakery, since you

are too young to **(8)** _____! Please send my

love to Ed and Emma, whom I **(9)** _____.

I am **(10)** _____ to see you all again!

Your loving niece,

Lydia Grace

TRY THIS! Create word pairs with the Vocabulary Words. You may pair each word with a synonym or with an antonym—for example, pair *vacant* with *empty* or with *full*.

Practice Book
Lead the Way

Name _____

▶ **Read the story. Then circle the letter of the best answer to each question.**

One afternoon in spring, Dawn was looking at the straight rows in Grandpa's garden. Suddenly she called, "Look! A bunny! Grandpa, it hopped right over your tomato plants."

"Oh, no," Grandpa groaned. "That rabbit is heading for my lettuce patch. It eats every lettuce leaf it can find. What can I do? I don't have enough wire to put a fence around the whole garden."

"I can solve your problem, Grandpa," Dawn promised.

The next morning Grandpa found Dawn making a pile of pulled dandelions in a corner of the garden. "What are you doing out here so early?" he asked.

"I'm making dandelion salad for the bunny, Grandpa. You don't need the weeds, and the rabbits like these as much as lettuce."

1 Who are the main characters?
  A Grandpa and a rabbit
  B Grandpa and a gardener
  C Dawn and Grandpa
  D Dawn and a rabbit

Tip Find the names of the most important characters in the story.

2 Where does the story happen?
  F in an apartment building
  G on a farm
  H in a park
  J in Grandpa's garden

Tip Look for words such as *in*, *on*, or *at* that tell where the story takes place.

3 What is Grandpa's problem?
  A Dawn doesn't help Grandpa.
  B Dawn doesn't like rabbits.
  C A rabbit is eating Grandpa's lettuce.
  D Grandpa grows too much lettuce.

Tip Notice that Grandpa signals his problem with the words *Oh, no* and *What can I do?*

© Harcourt

SCHOOL-HOME CONNECTION Help your child write a scene like the one above. Include characters, a setting, and a plot. When you're finished, have your child read the scene aloud.

2

Practice Book
Lead the Way

Name _____

▶ **Read the letter. Then write *Yes* or *No* after each statement to indicate whether a reader could correctly make that inference.**

Dear Aunt Eva,

We had a great time planting our garden today. We met at the empty lot. Some of us walked or rode bikes. Others came by car or bus. The sky was cloudy, but everyone felt cheerful.

I'm afraid that bringing Ruff was a mistake. He's a sweet dog, but he loves to dig and run. He even tried to jump over the fence! Liz grabbed him and brought him back to me. I kept Ruff on his leash after that.

Ms. Kwan gave us many kinds of seeds to plant. There were zinnias, sunflowers, marigolds, cosmos, and many more. We dug holes, dropped the seeds into the ground, and covered them up with dirt. I had the best job of all—using the hose to water the seeds. Ms. Kwan even brought some tulip and daffodil bulbs for us to plant!

When we finished planting, Ms. Kwan had a picnic ready for us. We all had a terrific day. I wish you could have been here! You would have loved it.

Love,

Anita

1. The children are going to sell the vegetables from the garden they planted.

_____

2. Liz and Anita are friends. _____

3. Anita's aunt likes planting flowers. _____

4. The garden is in Ms. Kwan's yard. _____

5. Anita likes to tell her aunt about her activities. _____

6. Ruff is Ms. Kwan's dog. _____

7. The children all live in the same neighborhood. _____

8. It didn't rain on the day they planted the garden. _____

9. At least four people helped plant the garden. _____

10. Anita and her aunt live in the same house _____

SCHOOL-HOME CONNECTION For each statement to which your child answered *Yes*, help him or her underline the parts of the letter that support this inference.

3

Practice Book
Lead the Way

© Harcourt

▶ **If the words form a sentence, write** *sentence*. **If not, think of words to make the sentence complete. Write the new sentence.**

1. Many people from the country.

_____

2. Made her uncle very happy.

_____

3. The cat slept on Lydia Grace's bed.

_____

4. She enjoys gardening.

_____

5. Uncle Jim's friend Emma.

_____

▶ **Rewrite these sentences. Begin and end them correctly.**

6. she planted seeds in cracked cups

_____

7. is her story a bit sad

_____

8. the girl left her family behind

_____

9. did she move to a strange place

_____

10. she seems very brave and clever

_____

© Harcourt

Practice Book
Lead the Way

Name _____

▶ **Read each sentence. Choose the answer that tells what the underlined word means. Circle the letter of the best answer.**

1 If you did <u>badly</u> on the quiz, be sure to study hard for the test.
  A less bad
  B in a bad way
  C not bad
  D bad again

2 We were <u>misinformed</u> about what time the game would start.
  F not given information
  G given too much information
  H given information again
  J given wrong information

3 He was <u>unsure</u> of the answer.
  A in a sure way
  B capable of being sure
  C not sure
  D too sure

4 The <u>fearless</u> bird flew very high.
  F full of fear
  G capable of fear
  H without fear
  J the state of having fear

5 Our teacher was <u>dissatisfied</u> with the test results.
  A more satisfied
  B less satisfied
  C satisfied again
  D the opposite of *satisfied*

6 <u>Dangerous</u> activities should be supervised.
  F full of danger
  G free from danger
  H with little danger
  J the opposite of *danger*

7 The chef <u>overcooked</u> the sauce.
  A cooked too much
  B did not cook enough
  C cooked again
  D the act of cooking

8 The directions were <u>understandable</u>.
  F hard to understand
  G the act of understanding
  H understood again
  J capable of being understood

© Harcourt

SCHOOL-HOME CONNECTION Play a game with word roots such as *sens* and *vis*. Say the root. Then have family members add prefixes and/or suffixes to form as many words as possible—for example: *sensory, insensitive; vision, invisible.*

7

Practice Book
Lead the Way

Name _____

▶ Choose two synonyms from the box for each word. Decide which one has a milder meaning and which one has a stronger meaning, and write them in the blank. An example has been done for you. Use each word only once.

| content | rude | terrified | cantankerous |
| boisterous | shy | stupendous | good |

	Milder Word		Stronger Word
1.	careful	picky	persnickety
2.	_____	quarrelsome	_____
3.	_____	cheerful	_____
4.	_____	great	_____
5.	_____	timid	_____

▶ Write an antonym for each underlined word.

6. They were <u>honest</u> to return the man's wallet. _____

7. He is <u>careful</u> with garden tools. _____

8. I always pick the <u>best</u> book to read. _____

9. She <u>reduces</u> the number of prizes we can win. _____

10. We were glad that the show was so <u>interesting</u>. _____

Practice Book
Lead the Way

© Harcourt

Name _____

▶ **Draw one line under each subject. Draw two lines under each predicate.**

1. I visited the Baseball Hall of Fame.

2. The museum has pictures of Lou Gehrig.

3. Some pictures show Babe Ruth, too.

4. Cooperstown is a wonderful place.

5. Many schoolchildren travel to the museum.

▶ **Add a subject or a predicate to complete each sentence.**

6. This baseball team _____.

7. _____ caught the ball.

8. _____ threw it to second base.

9. The runner _____.

10. _____ cheered in the stands.

TRY THIS! Write five sentences about a sport you like. Draw one line under the subject and two lines under the predicate in each sentence you write.

Practice Book
Lead the Way

© Harcourt

Name _____

Lou Gehrig: The
Luckiest Man

Spelling: Words
with Long and
Short o and u

Skill Reminder The long o sound can be spelled *o-e* or *oa*.
The short o sound is usually spelled *o*. The long *u* sound can
be spelled *u-e* or *ew*. The short *u* sound is usually spelled *u*.

▶ Fold the paper along the dotted line. As each
spelling word is read aloud, write it in the blank.
Then unfold your paper, and check your work.
Practice any spelling words you missed.

1. _____

2. _____

3. _____

4. _____

5. _____

6. _____

7. _____

8. _____

9. _____

10. _____

11. _____

12. _____

13. _____

14. _____

15. _____

16. _____

17. _____

18. _____

19. _____

20. _____

SPELLING WORDS

1. those
2. coach
3. solid
4. include
5. crew
6. plus
7. operate
8. broke
9. upset
10. tune
11. June
12. floating
13. plume
14. renew
15. husband
16. honor
17. smoke
18. conflict
19. stew
20. thunder

© Harcourt

Practice Book
Lead the Way

Name _____

▶ **Write the Vocabulary Word that best completes each sentence.**

outspoken	practical	elegant	elevations
starstruck	miniatures	brisk	marveled

1. Helen likes to take walks in the _____ evening air.

2. My friend Lucita is going to an _____ dinner party.

3. Karl uses a telescope to look at the _____ sky.

4. David collects _____ of famous buildings.

5. Isaiah _____ at the size of the redwood tree.

▶ **Write the Vocabulary Word that means the *opposite* of each word.**

6. depths _____

7. quiet _____

8. foolish _____

9. sloppy _____

10. warm _____

TRY THIS! Write a synonym for each Vocabulary Word in items 6–10.

Practice Book
Lead the Way

© Harcourt

Name _____

HOMEWORK
Amelia and
Eleanor Go for
a Ride
Locate Information
TEST PREP

▶ **Read the book parts, and use them to help you answer the questions on the following page.**

Book Cover

Famous Women

by Jane Wu

Table of Contents

Glossary

biplane: an airplane with two sets of
  wings, one above the other
First Lady: the wife of the President
  of the United States
scarlet fever: a disease that causes
  fever and a rash

Index

© Harcourt

Name _____

HOMEWORK
Amelia and
Eleanor Go for
a Ride
Locate Information
TEST PREP

▶ **Circle the letter of the best answer to each question.**

1 Where would you look to find out
what the term *First Lady* means?
   A the book cover
   B the table of contents
   C the glossary
   D the index

💡 **Tip**
What book part gives definitions
of terms?

2 On what page does the chapter
about Laura Ingalls Wilder begin?
   F page 3
   G page 39
   H page 72
   J page 104

💡 **Tip**
Where can you find information
about the chapters in the book?

3 What page or pages refer to
both Amelia Earhart and
Eleanor Roosevelt?
   A pages 3–38
   B pages 43–45
   C pages 27 and 39–71
   D pages 27 and 45

💡 **Tip**
Where would you look to find
out where someone or
something is mentioned in the
book? Remember to count all
pages in a range.

4 Where would you look to find
the name of the author of the
book?
   F the book cover
   G the table of contents
   H the glossary
   J the index

💡 **Tip**
Three book parts contain
names, so be careful.

SCHOOL-HOME CONNECTION With your child, look
at several tables of contents, glossaries, or indexes in
books or magazines. Help your child practice looking
for specific information.

Practice Book
Lead the Way

© Harcourt

Name _____

Amelia and
Eleanor Go for
a Ride

Grammar:
Complete and
Simple Subjects

▶ **Draw one line under each complete subject. Then circle each simple subject.**

1. Many kinds of hobbies are popular nowadays.

2. Some people like to take classes to learn new things.

3. My best friend likes to play sports in her spare time.

4. Computer games are a new hobby that many people enjoy.

5. My cousin likes to build models from kits.

▶ **Add a complete subject to complete each sentence. Circle each simple subject.**

6. _____ learned how to fly.

7. _____ traveled to Europe and Africa.

8. _____ met the President of the United States.

9. _____ talked to people from around the world.

10. _____ was the most amazing sight.

11. _____ seemed to last forever.

12. _____ danced gracefully.

22

Name _____

Amelia and
Eleanor Go for
a Ride

Spelling: Words
with /o͞o/

Skill Reminder The /o͞o/ sound can be spelled *oo* or *ou*.

▶ Fold the paper along the dotted line. As each
spelling word is read aloud, write it in the blank.
Then unfold your paper, and check your work.
Practice any spelling words you missed.

1. _____
2. _____
3. _____
4. _____
5. _____
6. _____
7. _____
8. _____
9. _____
10. _____
11. _____
12. _____
13. _____
14. _____
15. _____
16. _____
17. _____
18. _____
19. _____
20. _____

SPELLING WORDS

1. loop
2. wounded
3. shoot
4. booth
5. broom
6. boost
7. mood
8. fooling
9. afternoon
10. room
11. smooth
12. tooth
13. raccoon
14. bloomed
15. souvenir
16. routine
17. roofs
18. loose
19. coop
20. stoop

23

Practice Book
Lead the Way

▶ Read the Vocabulary Words. Then read the group of
synonyms for each word. Write the Vocabulary Word that
has nearly the same meaning as the group of words.

| privilege | luxury | shiftless | assent |
| shamefacedly | elated | indignantly | ad-lib |

1. lazy
slow
doing-nothing

_____

5. right
freedom

_____

2. excited
happy
thrilled

_____

6. treat
pleasure
comfort

_____

3. make up
invent
create

_____

7. uncomfortably
with embarrassment
guiltily

_____

4. agreement
approval

_____

8. angrily
unpleasantly

_____

Name _____

▶ **Read the passage. Then circle the letter of the best answer to each question.**

Because conditions were just right, more than a foot of snow fell last night. This morning there was a lot of shoveling to do, so my sister and I decided to see whether our neighbors needed help shoveling. We looked down the street and saw that Mrs. Hartman was still snowed in. We didn't know Mrs. Hartman very well, but we decided to clear her sidewalk and driveway. After we were finished, she invited us in for a cup of cocoa. As we said good-bye, the three of us agreed that we were lucky to have had so much snow. If there hadn't been a storm, then we might not have gotten to know each other!

1 Why was the amount of the snowfall so great?

  A No one had a shovel.

  B Conditions were just right.

  C It was the biggest storm in ten years.

  D The neighbors needed help shoveling.

> 💡 **Tip**
> Which answer choice describes the cause of the huge snowfall?

2 What was one of the effects of the snowstorm?

  F The neighbors next door borrowed a shovel.

  G There was no school for a week.

  H The children got to know one of their neighbors.

  J No one had to go to work the next day.

> 💡 **Tip**
> Ignore answers that are not in the passage.

3 Which of the following does NOT signal a cause-and-effect relationship?

  A after all

  B so

  C because

  D if/then

> 💡 **Tip**
> Which of the answer choices best signals a closing line?

© Harcourt

SCHOOL-HOME CONNECTION With your child, explore cause-and-effect relationships in everyday events at school or at home. Link these events, using signal words like *because, since, so,* and *as a result.*

Practice Book
Lead the Way

Name _____

▶ **Authors use figurative language, such as similes and metaphors, to make their writing more interesting. Rewrite each of the sentences below, using a simile or a metaphor. Remember, a simile compares two things, using the word *like* or *as*. A metaphor compares two things by saying that one thing *is* another.**

Ordinary Language	Figurative Language
1. Manuel spoke angrily to them. (simile)	1. _____
2. Pablo sniffed the air. (simile)	2. _____
3. Pablo had a bright smile. (metaphor)	3. _____
4. He liked the smell of the pastries. (metaphor)	4. _____
5. Pablo inhaled and closed his eyes. (simile)	5. _____
6. Pablo smiled when he saw Carlos and the girls. (simile)	6. _____
7. The children crowded around the counter. (simile)	7. _____
8. The tray was stacked with pastries. (metaphor)	8. _____

© Harcourt

SCHOOL-HOME CONNECTION With your child, create similes and metaphors to describe sights, sounds, and smells in your neighborhood.

26

Practice Book
Lead the Way

The Baker's
Neighbor

Grammar:
Complete
and Simple
Predicates

Name _____

▶ **Draw one line under the complete predicate. Then circle
the simple predicate.**

    1. Pablo smelled the freshly baked pies and cakes.

    2. Manuel counted all his money.

    3. The children crowded around the counter.

    4. Manuel snorted in disgust.

▶ **Add a complete predicate to each subject. Circle the simple predicate in
each complete predicate you write.**

    5. The baker _____.

    6. The pies and cakes _____.

    _____.

    7. All three women _____.

    8. Carlos' sisters _____.

    9. The gold coins _____.

   10. The villagers and children _____.

 TRY THIS! Write three sentences that give examples of people being good neighbors.
Circle the simple predicate in each sentence you write.

Practice Book
Lead the Way

Name _____

Skill Reminder   The vowel sound you hear in *are* and *car* is
usually spelled with *ar*.

▶ Fold the paper along the dotted line. As each
spelling word is read aloud, write it in the blank.
Then unfold your paper, and check your work.
Practice any spelling words you missed.

1. _____

2. _____

3. _____

4. _____

5. _____

6. _____

7. _____

8. _____

9. _____

10. _____

11. _____

12. _____

13. _____

14. _____

15. _____

16. _____

17. _____

18. _____

19. _____

20. _____

SPELLING WORDS

1. carved
2. garden
3. harm
4. farther
5. barked
6. alarm
7. chart
8. starved
9. harder
10. parked
11. smartest
12. charge
13. guard
14. argument
15. hardware
16. garbage
17. harsh
18. parts
19. radar
20. harbor

Practice Book
Lead the Way

© Harcourt

The Emperor and
the Kite

Grammar:
Compound
Subjects and
Predicates

▶ **Draw one line under each simple subject. Draw two lines
under each simple predicate. Label each sentence** *compound
subject* **or** *compound predicate*.

1. Every year, Jake and Katie go to a
   kite-flying contest at school. _____

2. The students and the teachers gather
   on the soccer field to watch the kites. _____

3. Katie's kite dances and swirls through
   the air. _____

4. The principal chooses the best kite
   and gives the award. _____

5. Jake and his friend Kinuko fly their
   kites longer than anyone else. _____

6. The winning kite is the biggest
   and soars the highest. _____

▶ **Rewrite these sentences. Add commas where they are needed.**

7. Last week, Katie made a kite attached some string to it and flew it in the park.

   _____

   _____

8. I think Katie Jaime and their friend Samir have the prettiest kites.

   _____

9. They have fun win prizes and show off their kites.

   _____

10. When they arrive home, their mother father and little brother cheer for them.

   _____

   _____

© Harcourt

| **Skill Reminder** | The /ôr/ sound can be spelled *our, or,* or *ore.* |

▶ Fold the paper along the dotted line. As each spelling word is read aloud, write it in the blank. Then unfold your paper, and check your work. Practice any spelling words you missed.

1. _____
2. _____
3. _____
4. _____
5. _____
6. _____
7. _____
8. _____
9. _____
10. _____
11. _____
12. _____
13. _____
14. _____
15. _____
16. _____
17. _____
18. _____
19. _____
20. _____

SPELLING WORDS

1. pour
2. orbit
3. fourth
4. source
5. sports
6. forward
7. force
8. order
9. wore
10. yourself
11. support
12. sore
13. orange
14. anymore
15. ignore
16. portrait
17. border
18. course
19. tornado
20. your

© Harcourt

Name _____

▶ **Write the answer to each question.**

1. If you wanted to find out how flamingos care for their young, in which encyclopedia volume would you look?

_____

2. If you wanted to find the most recent list of endangered animals, would it be better to look in a print encyclopedia or on the Internet?

_____

3. Why?

_____

_____

▶ **Write the keywords you would use to perform an Internet search to answer each question.**

4. What kind of nest do ospreys build?

_____ AND _____

5. What birds would you see in California?

_____ AND _____

SCHOOL-HOME CONNECTION Talk with your child about a bird or another animal that interests both of you. Make a list of questions you have about the creature. Together with your child, list some keywords that could be used to search for the information on the Internet.

35

Practice Book
Lead the Way

© Harcourt

Name _____

▶ **Identify each word group as a *comma splice* or *run-on sentence*. Then rewrite each one correctly as a compound sentence.**

1. Halla has a flashlight she is carrying a box. _____

_____

2. The bird fell, Halla saved it. _____

_____

▶ **Rewrite each pair of sentences as a compound sentence, using the conjunction in parentheses ( ).**

3. The birds are slow. They move well in water. **(but)**

_____

_____

4. Halla loves puffins. She helps them each year. **(and)**

_____

_____

5. Children climb the cliffs. They watch the puffins. **(and)**

_____

_____

6. The puffins ignore them. They hide in holes. **(or)**

_____

_____

 TRY THIS! Write three compound sentences about an unusual animal. Use each of the conjunctions *and, or,* and *but* once.

Skill Reminder   The /âr/ sound can be spelled *are*, *air*, or *ere*.

▶ Fold the paper along the dotted line. As each spelling word is read aloud, write it in the blank. Then unfold your paper, and check your work. Practice any spelling words you missed.

1. _____

2. _____

3. _____

4. _____

5. _____

6. _____

7. _____

8. _____

9. _____

10. _____

11. _____

12. _____

13. _____

14. _____

15. _____

16. _____

17. _____

18. _____

19. _____

20. _____

SPELLING WORDS

1. cared
2. dairy
3. unfair
4. rarely
5. stared
6. dared
7. glare
8. airplanes
9. barely
10. farewell
11. software
12. staircase
13. everywhere
14. declare
15. square
16. therefore
17. despair
18. prepared
19. beware
20. repair

© Harcourt

Practice Book
Lead the Way

▶ **Read the Vocabulary Words. Then write the Vocabulary Word that answers each riddle. Use each word twice.**

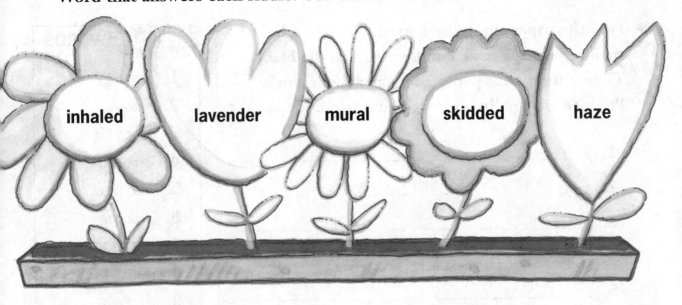

inhaled   lavender   mural   skidded   haze

1. I am a shade of purple.
   What color am I?   _____

2. I was running fast. When I stopped
   quickly, I slid. What did I do?   _____

3. I did this when I took air into my body.
   What did I do?   _____

4. I can make it hard to see.
   What am I?   _____

5. I am a very large picture made by
   one or more artists. What am I?   _____

6. I am like a fog.
   What am I?   _____

7. I'm a plant as well as a color.
   What am I?   _____

8. I mean "breathed in."
   What word am I?   _____

9. I am art that is painted on a wall.
   What am I?   _____

10. When I stopped my bike, I left tire
    marks on the road. What did I do?   _____

Name _____

Skill Reminder cause = why something happens

effect = what happens

▶ **Read the story. Circle the letter of the best answer to each question.**

Last spring the principal of Beech Street School gave our school a challenge. He asked us to find ways to make the school a better place. The fourth-grade class decided to plant a garden. The class cleared land behind the school. Students asked for community help, so the hardware store donated free seeds. Students planted seeds and carefully watered and cared for the young plants. Finally, their work paid off. In the spring students picked more than 10 pounds of vegetables. Because they had enough food to share, the fourth graders held a picnic for the whole school.

1 What was the direct effect of the principal's challenge?
   A The principal wanted to make the school a better place.
   B Fourth graders decided to plant a garden.
   C Students went to a picnic.
   D The plants grew large.

Tip
Remember that an effect is what happens because of another event.

2 Why did the hardware store donate seeds?
   F The principal asked for them.
   G Students wanted to plant a garden.
   H Students asked for community help.
   J Students held a picnic.

Tip
Find the signal word *so* to help you to see the cause-and-effect relationship.

3 What caused the fourth graders to hold a picnic?
   A They had enough food to share.
   B It was the last day of school.
   C They wanted to make the school a better place.
   D The principal gave a challenge.

Tip
A cause is why something happens. Find the sentence that tells why the fourth graders held the picnic.

SCHOOL-HOME CONNECTION Talk with your child about three things he or she did today. List one effect for each action.

39

Practice Book
Lead the Way

© Harcourt

Name _____

▶ **Find the independent and dependent clauses in these sentences. Draw one line under each independent clause. Draw two lines under each dependent clause.**

1. After Mrs. Willie Mae Washington and Mr. Singh told her about the Garden of Happiness, Marisol decided to plant something, too.

2. When Marisol planted a seed, it grew into a tall plant.

3. Marisol was happy because her sunflower was so beautiful.

4. Because she loved sweet potato pie, Mrs. Willie Mae Washington planted sweet potatoes.

▶ **Rewrite each sentence. Add the kind of clause named in parentheses ( ). Remember to add commas as needed.**

5. The teenagers painted a mural _____

_____. **(dependent)**

6. After the neighbors prepared the ground _____

_____. **(independent)**

7. _____

because Marisol wanted to plant something in the Garden of Happiness.
(independent)

8. _____

Mr. Singh planted beans. **(dependent)**

TRY THIS! Identify dependent clauses in "The Garden of Happiness." Change them into independent clauses. Then identify independent clauses, and change them into dependent clauses.

Practice Book
Lead the Way

Name _____

Skill Reminder   summary = main idea + details

▶ **Read the paragraphs. Then circle the letter of the best answer to each question below.**

Prairie dogs live in underground towns made up of rooms connected by tunnels. Some rooms are for sleeping, and others are for storing food. Some are nurseries, where young prairie dogs are raised. These towns include listening posts above ground. There, the prairie dogs listen for enemies.

When a prairie dog hears an enemy, it barks to warn others to hide. This barking noise gave the prairie dog its name, but the animal isn't really a dog. It is a type of ground squirrel. Sometimes prairie dogs stand on their hind legs, throw their heads back, and give a whistling call. They may be letting other prairie dogs know that this is their territory.

1 Which of these sentences is the main idea of the first paragraph?
  A Prairie dogs make a lot of noise.
  B Prairie dogs take good care of their young.
  C Prairie dogs can stand on their hind legs.
  D Prairie dogs live in underground towns.

> **Tip**
> Ignore choices not found in the paragraph.

2 Which of these sentences supports the main idea of the first paragraph?
  F Prairie dogs sometimes make whistling sounds.
  G Prairie dog towns have different rooms that are used for different activities.
  H Prairie dogs can bark.
  J Prairie dogs do not get along.

> **Tip**
> Look for the sentence that explains in a general way all the details in the first paragraph.

3 Which of these sentences summarizes the second paragraph?
  A Prairie dogs make different sounds to communicate with other prairie dogs.
  B Prairie dog towns have listening posts.
  C Prairie dogs are quiet animals.
  D The prairie dog is a type of ground squirrel.

> **Tip**
> Which sentence combines the main idea and the most important details of the second paragraph?

SCHOOL-HOME CONNECTION With your child, discuss ways people help one another. Then help your child create a list of ways he or she has helped someone in the past.

43

© Harcourt

Name _____

▶ Label each sentence *simple*, *compound*, or *complex*.

1. Orangutans are sweet, but they have sharp

teeth. _____

2. When I met Nanang, he

was very young. _____

3. Nanang will return to the forest. _____

4. After he returns to the forest, my job is done.

_____

▶ Draw one line under each independent clause. Draw two lines
under each dependent clause.

5. Since Nanang does not have his mother, he needs the babysitter.

6. Although he is young, he is quite strong.

▶ Combine each pair of sentences into a complex sentence.
The connecting words in the box may help you.

after	because	if	when
although	before	since	while

7. Nanang held my hand. We walked in the forest.

_____

_____

8. Nanang is so young. He is in danger from snakes.

_____

_____

Practice Book
Lead the Way

© Harcourt

Name _____

PRAIRIE FLOWERS

5. About what percent of the prairie flowers are prairie violets?

_____

6. About what percent of the prairie flowers are neither prairie violets nor bride's

bonnets? _____

7. What do you call the part of the paddock that keeps the horses from running

away? _____

8. Where would the horses run in order to escape a rainstorm? _____

SCHOOL-HOME CONNECTION With your child, draw a diagram of a room in your home. Label where the furniture is placed.

Practice Book
Lead the Way

© Harcourt

Name _____

▶ Write *common* or *proper* to identify each underlined noun.

1. The <u>sheep</u> ran in the field. _____

2. As we waited, <u>Caleb</u> played with a marble. _____

3. Suddenly he saw a yellow <u>bonnet</u>. _____

4. Papa's wagon was pulled by <u>Jack</u> and Old Bess. _____

5. Sarah brought <u>Seal</u>, a gray cat with white feet. _____

▶ For each sentence, fill in the blank with a common noun.

6. We watched the wagon with _____ in our hearts.

7. The wagon passed the _____ and then stopped.

8. One of Sarah's gifts was a(n) _____.

9. Sarah told my _____, Caleb, about gulls.

10. Sarah's room had a(n) _____ in it.

▶ Complete each sentence by writing a proper noun in the blank.

11. Before he left, _____ combed his hair.

12. Sarah gave Caleb's sister, _____, a sea stone.

13. Did the stone really come from the state of _____?

14. Lottie and _____ stared at Sarah's cat.

15. _____ stepped out of her case and purred.

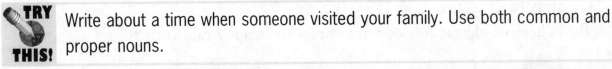

TRY THIS! Write about a time when someone visited your family. Use both common and proper nouns.

© Harcourt

Practice Book
Lead the Way

Name _____

▶ **Rewrite each sentence, replacing the underlined word or
words with a pronoun. Write *subject* or *object* to identify
each pronoun you use.**

1. <u>Chester</u> made earmuffs for everyone. _____

   _____

2. Mr. Parsons told Josh about <u>David Potter</u>. _____

   _____

3. <u>Josh and David</u> worked together to design a glove. _____

   _____

4. Soon David played for <u>the Spring Branch Mustangs.</u> _____

   _____

5. <u>Reeba Daniel</u> invented a washer/dryer. _____

   _____

6. <u>Reeba's invention</u> won a prize. _____

   _____

▶ **Rewrite each sentence. Correct any errors in the use of pronouns.**

7. Josh and me helped David. _____

   _____

8. David thanked me and Josh for helping. _____

   _____

**TRY
THIS!** Write three separate sentences about an invention that you find useful.
Then put your sentences together in a paragraph, using pronouns to
replace nouns as needed.

© Harcourt

Name _____

The Kids'
Invention Book

Spelling: Words
That End with
-y or -ey

Skill Reminder   The long e sound at the end of a word can be spelled y or ey.

▶ Fold the paper along the dotted line. As each spelling word is read aloud, write it in the blank. Then unfold your paper, and check your work. Practice any spelling words you missed.

1. _____
2. _____
3. _____
4. _____
5. _____
6. _____
7. _____
8. _____
9. _____
10. _____
11. _____
12. _____
13. _____
14. _____
15. _____
16. _____
17. _____
18. _____
19. _____
20. _____

SPELLING WORDS

1. tiny
2. hockey
3. heavy
4. every
5. money
6. turkey
7. early
8. hungry
9. already
10. valley
11. nobody
12. monkey
13. company
14. country
15. ability
16. steady
17. everybody
18. industry
19. activity
20. honey

© Harcourt

Name _____

▶ **Write the Vocabulary Word that matches each clue.**

muttered	strengthening	sculptor
straightaway	retorted	alibi

1. giving more energy to

2. one who makes statues

3. talked in a low voice

4. answered back

5. an excuse given by one accused

6. immediately

▶ **Write the Vocabulary Word that means the *opposite* of each word below.**

7. asked _____

8. weakening _____

9. shouted _____

10. later _____

TRY THIS! Describe a time when you looked for something you lost. Tell what happened, using three Vocabulary Words.

© Harcourt

73

Name _____

HOMEWORK
The Case of
Pablo's Nose
Sequence
TEST PREP

▶ **Read the paragraph. Then circle the letter of the best answer to each question.**

Jamal's Story

Last week, my dad and I went to a baseball game. First, my dad bought me a hot dog. Then, we handed over our tickets and went to our seats. Once we sat down, we read our programs. It was fun reading about the players. After that, my dad bought me a second hot dog. It tasted great! Next, we decided to walk around for a while before the game started. Later, a man came onto the field to sing the national anthem. Finally, the pitcher walked out, and the game began.

1 What is the second thing Jamal and his father did when they went to the baseball game?

  A They went to their seats.
  B They met the players.
  C They read their programs.
  D They handed over their tickets.

> 💡**Tip**
> Begin by finding the first thing Jamal did with his father when they went to the baseball game.

2 What did they do after Jamal's father bought Jamal a second hot dog?

  F They sang the national anthem.
  G They walked around for a while.
  H They handed over their tickets.
  J They bought programs.

> 💡**Tip**
> Look for a time-order word to help you.

3 What did Jamal and his father do right after they went to their seats?

  A They read their programs.
  B They bought tickets.
  C They walked around for a while.
  D They played baseball.

> 💡**Tip**
> Ignore the answer choice that is clearly wrong.

 SCHOOL-HOME CONNECTION Help your child write a set of directions that explain how to do a common household chore. Then try to perform the chore, using your child's directions.

Practice Book
Lead the Way

© Harcourt

Name _____

▶ **Write the possessive pronouns that could replace each group of words below.**

	Before a Noun	Not Before a Noun
1. Martha Katz's	_____	_____
2. the townspeople's	_____	_____
3. belonging to me	_____	_____
4. Pablo's	_____	_____
5. owned by Sally and me	_____	_____

▶ **Rewrite each sentence, replacing the underlined words with possessive pronouns.**

6. Pablo did not ride <u>Pablo's</u> bike to Encyclopedia's house.

_____

7. Pablo and Sally had almost made up <u>Pablo's and Sally's</u> minds.

_____

8. Sally eagerly gave Encyclopedia <u>Sally's</u> opinion.

_____

9. "Yes, that bike is <u>Desmoana's</u>," admitted Desmoana at last.

_____

10. "You and I make a great team, Sally," Encyclopedia said. "The credit for solving this case is <u>Sally's and Encyclopedia's</u>."

_____

TRY THIS! What are some of your favorite things? Use possessive pronouns to write five sentences about the items. Include examples of both kinds of possessive pronouns.

© Harcourt

Name _____

Skill Reminder   The prefix *un-* or *dis-* at the beginning of a word means "not." For most words, no spelling changes are needed when adding *un-* or *dis-*.

▶ Fold the paper along the dotted line. As each spelling word is read aloud, write it in the blank. Then unfold your paper, and check your work. Practice any spelling words you missed.

1. _____
2. _____
3. _____
4. _____
5. _____
6. _____
7. _____
8. _____
9. _____
10. _____
11. _____
12. _____
13. _____
14. _____
15. _____
16. _____
17. _____
18. _____
19. _____
20. _____

SPELLING WORDS

1. unused
2. dislike
3. unclean
4. unheard
5. disagree
6. disabled
7. unkind
8. unfriendly
9. unable
10. unhappy
11. unsafe
12. disobey
13. uncertain
14. disappear
15. undecided
16. dishonest
17. disadvantage
18. distrust
19. unknown
20. unlike

© Harcourt

76

Name _____

HOMEWO█
In the Day █f
King Ad██ █
Folk Liter█ █ure
and My█ █s

► **Read the following Korean folktale. Then answer the questions.**

The Judge and the Young Boy

Once there lived a dishonest judge. One of the officers in his court was a g██od and honest man whom the judge didn't like, so the judge came up with a pla█ to get rid of him. During a winter snowstorm, the judge called the honest offic█ in. "I have a craving for fresh peaches and strawberries. Go out and find me so█ █. If you return with them in less than a month, you'll receive a generous rewar█ If you do not, you will lose your job."

The honest officer knew he couldn't find fresh fruits in the winter, but h█ █ade a great effort anyway. After days of searching in the bitter cold, he became i█ █nd returned home. The officer's young son asked him where he had been and █ █at he had been doing out in the snowstorm.

After hearing his father's story, the young boy went straight to the dish█ █st judge. "Sir," he said to the judge, "my father was bitten by a poisonous sn█ █."

"You lie!" shouted the judge. "No snakes would be out in this heavy wint█ snow!"

"Yet," the boy said calmly, "you sent my father out to find fresh peach█ █and strawberries. Perhaps you should take back your order, and my father sh█ █d take back his job."

The judge was stunned and speechless.

Not long afterward, the governor of the district replaced the dishones█ █udge with the young boy's father. He ruled wisely for many years.

1. What is the lesson of this folktale?

_____

_____

2. Do you believe that the lesson in this folktale is important only to █orean people? Explain your answer.

_____

_____

SCHOOL-HOME CONNECTION Tell your child a folktale, myth, or fable that you remember from your own childhood. Then share ideas about the main idea or lesson of the tale. Have your child write down the main idea in a single sentence.

79

© Harcourt

Name _____

▶ **Rewrite each sentence. Replace the blank with an adjective of the type in parentheses ( ).**

1. The visitors described the _____ dreams. **(how many?)**

   _____

   _____

2. It was a(n) _____ evening. **(what kind?)**

   _____

   _____

3. The woman cooked _____ meal. **(which one?)**

   _____

   _____

4. Did _____ travelers learn a lesson? **(which ones?)**

   _____

   _____

5. This was quite a(n) _____ adventure. **(what kind?)**

   _____

   _____

▶ **Rewrite each sentence, using the correct article in parentheses ( ).**

6. **(A, The)** travelers arrived at **(a, the)** old woman's house.

   _____

7. Did they enjoy **(a, an)** exciting meal?

   _____

8. **(An, The)** ham was **(a, an)** big surprise!

   _____

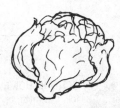

Practice Book
Lead the Way

© Harcourt

Name _____

Skill Reminder The prefix *non-* or *in-* can mean "not."
The prefix *re-* means "again."

▶ Fold the paper along the dotted line. As each
spelling word is read aloud, write it in the blank.
Then unfold your paper, and check your work.
Practice any spelling words you missed.

1. _____
2. _____
3. _____
4. _____
5. _____
6. _____
7. _____
8. _____
9. _____
10. _____
1. _____
_____
1 _____
14 _____
15. _____
16. _____
17. _____
18. _____
19. _____
20. _____

SPELLING WORDS

1. nonstop
2. replaced
3. inactive
4. refill
5. incorrect
6. rethink
7. nonfat
8. reread
9. retell
10. return
11. incomplete
12. repay
13. nonfiction
14. nonsense
15. indirect
16. independent
17. invisible
18. nonprofit
19. redo
20. relocate

Practice Book
Lead the Way

Name _____

▶ **Write the Vocabulary Word that best completes each sentence.**

script	triumphantly	desperately	injustice
repentant	acceptable	discards	circumstances

Blue Grass is **(1)** _____ eager to become a famous singer and songwriter. He wants to make people

happy with his music, so he **(2)** _____ any sad songs. Those that remain, he feels, should be

(3) _____ to any audience under all

(4) _____.

Then one day he whoops **(5)** _____. He has gotten an offer to write a song to go with a movie

(6) _____! However, it turns out that the movie producers want a sad song—what an

(7) _____! He accepts the movie offer anyway, but whenever he hears his song played, he feels

(8) _____.

TRY THIS! Write a new ending for one of your favorite fairy tales. Use at least three Vocabulary Words.

© Harcourt

Name _____

Skill Reminder **Look for time-order words to give you clues about the order in which events happen.**

▶ **Read the story. Then circle the letter of the best answer to each question.**

After a long morning of work, a thirsty ant went down to the river to get a drink. Before the ant could take a drink, it slipped on the riverbank and fell into the water. The next thing the ant knew, it was being carried down the river. While perched on a branch hanging over the water, a dove spotted the ant. When the dove saw that the ant was about to drown, the bird pulled a leaf off the branch and dropped it into the river. As soon as the ant reached the leaf, it climbed onto it. Then it floated to safety on the riverbank. There the ant rested under the tree where the dove sat. A little later, a bird-catcher came and began to lay a twig trap under the tree for the dove. When the ant saw what the bird-catcher was planning to do, it bit the bird-catcher's foot. The bird-catcher immediately cried out in pain and threw the twigs on the ground. The moment the dove heard the noise, it flew to the safety of another tree. The moral of the story is *One good deed deserves another.*

1 What happened before the ant could get a drink?
   A It sat under a tree.   **C** It worked all day.
   B It fell into the water.   **D** It climbed on the leaf.

Tip
Look in the story for the time-order word *before*.

2 When did the dove spot the ant?
   A after flying to another tree
   B when the bird-catcher set the trap
   C after dropping the leaf in the water
   D while sitting on a branch over the river

Tip
Find the word *spotted*. Then look at the rest of the sentence.

3 What happened right after the ant climbed onto the leaf?
   A It saw the bird-catcher.   **C** It floated to safety.
   B It started to drown.   **D** It stung the bird-catcher.

Tip
Which time-order word signals what the ant did after climbing on the leaf?

SCHOOL-HOME CONNECTION Talk with your child about the steps in making your child's favorite meal. Use time-order words in your discussion.

Practice Book
Lead the Way

© Harcourt

▶ **Rewrite each sentence, using the correct form of the
adjective in parentheses ( ).**

1. Red whistled a _____ tune. **(joyful)**

_____

2. It was a _____ tune than the one she whistled yesterday. **(happy)**

_____

3. In fact, it was the _____ tune she had whistled all week. **(nice)**

_____

4. The wolf was looking forward to a _____ treat. **(tasty)**

_____

5. "These are the _____ berries I've ever had," he grinned. **(fine)**

_____

6. "Strawberries are _____ than blueberries," he declared. **(sweet)**

_____

▶ **Complete each sentence by writing the
correct form of *good* in the blank.**

7. Making the wolf a ballet dancer

was _____ than having
him visit Grandma's house.

8. Miss Muffet thought the new

ending was the _____
she had heard.

Imagine that your three favorite story characters could meet. Write a
conversation they might have. Use several adjectives that compare.

84

© Harcourt

Skill Reminder   When a word ends with a consonant and
y, change y to *i* before adding *-es, -ed, -er, -est,* or *-ly*.

▶ Fold the paper along the dotted line. As each
spelling word is read aloud, write it in the blank.
Then unfold your paper, and check your work.
Practice any spelling words you missed.

1. _____
2. _____
3. _____
4. _____
5. _____
6. _____
7. _____
8. _____
9. _____
10. _____
11. _____
12. _____
13. _____
14. _____
15. _____
16. _____
17. _____
18. _____
19. _____
20. _____

SPELLING WORDS

1. families
2. worried
3. ugliest
4. funnier
5. happily
6. easily
7. heavier
8. earlier
9. tiniest
10. supplied
11. luckily
12. relied
13. activities
14. countries
15. enemies
16. scurried
17. libraries
18. prettier
19. readily
20. carried

© Harcourt

Practice Book
Lead the Way

85

Name _____

▶ **Write the Vocabulary Word that best completes each analogy.**

| decreed | famine | implored | trickle | plentifully |

1. *Singer* is to *chanted* as *beggar* is to _____.

2. *Reward* is to *punishment* as *feast* is to _____.

3. *Teacher* is to *instructed* as *king* is to _____.

4. *Enormous* is to *tiny* as *flood* is to _____.

5. *Quick* is to *quickly* as *plentiful* is to _____.

▶ **Write the Vocabulary Word that matches each clue.**

6. This happens when there is no food. _____

7. A judge did this. _____

8. It's how generous people give gifts. _____

9. Someone in need did this. _____

10. Water in a mostly dried-up stream did this. _____

 TRY THIS! Make up your own folktale about a grain of rice. Use at least two of the Vocabulary Words.

© Harcourt

Name _____

| **Skill Reminder** | • compare = tell how things are alike
• contrast = tell how things are different |

▶ **Read the paragraph. Then circle the letter of the best answer to each question.**

You may think that an elephant is an elephant. The fact is, there are two very distinct types—Asian and African. Asian and African elephants have many things in common. Both species of elephants have long trunks, thick legs, huge heads, and little body hair. On the other hand, there are noticeable differences. The African elephant is much larger and has much larger ears than the Asian elephant. Only male Asian elephants have tusks, but both male and female African elephants have tusks.

1 How are Asian and African elephants similar?
   A Only male Asian elephants have tusks.
   B The African elephant is larger.
   C Both have long trunks and huge heads.
   D Neither have large ears.

💡 **Tip**
The words *both* and *neither* signal that two things are alike.

2 Which of the following features are NOT the same for both Asian and African elephants?
   F long trunks
   G size of body and ears
   H little body hair
   J thick legs

💡 **Tip**
Which feature is different for the two elephant species?

3 Which words or phrase from the passage points out how Asian and African elephants are alike?
   A in common
   B On the other hand
   C Only
   D differences

💡 **Tip**
Find each answer choice in the passage. Pick the one that signals how things are alike.

SCHOOL-HOME CONNECTION With your child, choose two objects to compare and contrast. Have your child draw a Venn diagram. Discuss how the objects you chose are alike and different, and have your child fill in the diagram.

Practice Book
Lead the Way

© Harcourt

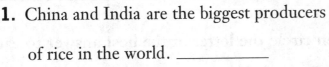

▶ **Underline the complete predicate in each sentence, and circle the verb. On the line, write *action* or *being* to describe the verb.**

1. China and India are the biggest producers

   of rice in the world. _____

2. Farmers in Arkansas, California, Texas, and

   Louisiana grow a lot of rice, too. _____

3. Rice plants thrive in 4 to 8 inches of water. _____

4. Actually, rice is the fruit of a type of grass. _____

5. Harvesters remove rice grains from the plant. _____

6. At the mill, workers process the rice. _____

▶ **Underline the verb or verb group in each sentence. Then write a new sentence using the verb or verb group you underlined.**

7. Bran, a thin brown skin, covers rice. _____

   _____

8. Brown rice has many vitamins and minerals. _____

   _____

9. The bran is removed at the mill. _____

   _____

10. The kernels are polished for white rice. _____

    _____

TRY THIS! Rani used mathematics to help him feed people. Write five sentences about other ways people use mathematics. Underline your verbs.

© Harcourt

Name _____

▶ **Underline the main verb. Circle the helping verb.**

1. The people have opened the hydrant.

2. Water is pouring all over the ground.

3. Their game could prove dangerous.

4. Perhaps the water will dry up.

5. Then any fire would cause great damage.

▶ **Complete each sentence with a verb from the box. Then circle the helping verb.**

| take | deserve | extinguished | relaxing | answer |

6. The firefighters were _____.

7. They had _____ a fire early that morning.

8. They do _____ a break now.

9. One firefighter will _____ the phones.

10. The rest should _____ a nap.

TRY THIS! On a separate sheet of paper, write five sentences about fighting fires. Use one of these helping verbs in each sentence: *were, could, does, has, will.*

© Harcourt

Practice Book
Lead the Way

Skill Reminder Some words end with an unaccented
syllable pronounced /ər/. The /ər/ sound can be spelled *or*, *ar*, or *er*.

▶ Fold the paper along the dotted line. As each
spelling word is read aloud, write it in the blank.
Then unfold your paper, and check your work.
Practice any spelling words you missed.

1. _____

2. _____

3. _____

4. _____

5. _____

6. _____

7. _____

8. _____

9. _____

10. _____

11. _____

12. _____

13. _____

14. _____

15. _____

16. _____

17. _____

18. _____

19. _____

20. _____

SPELLING WORDS

1. doctor
2. dollar
3. power
4. sugar
5. corner
6. collar
7. danger
8. ladder
9. labor
10. cellar
11. other
12. motor
13. hunger
14. calendar
15. horror
16. officer
17. finger
18. director
19. master
20. regular

Practice Book
Lead the Way

Name _____

▶ **Read the paragraph. Use one or more test-taking strategies from the box to help you circle the correct answer to each question. Then write the letters of the strategies you used.**

A passport is a document that allows citizens to travel to other countries and then return to their own country. United States passports are issued by the government. They are good for ten years for adults and five years for children. They must then be renewed. People show their passports when they first enter a country and when they are leaving. They usually must show their passports when they exchange money at a foreign bank. Passports are an important form of identification.

A. Find and use key words.   **B. Eliminate wrong or silly answers.**
C. Look back over the paragraph.

1. What is a passport?   Strategy: _____
   (a document used by travelers   a form of foreign money)

2. After how long must children renew their passports?   Strategy: _____
   (five years   ten years)

3. Why must foreign travelers keep their passports safe?   Strategy: _____
   (to buy souvenirs   to identify themselves)

▶ **Write the strategies in the order in which they should be followed.**

Return to the questions I skipped.   Look over the whole test.
Read the directions carefully.   Answer the questions I know first.
Check my answers.

1. First: _____

2. Next: _____

3. Then: _____

4. Then: _____

5. Last: _____

SCHOOL-HOME CONNECTION Discuss with your child the importance of getting enough sleep and eating a good breakfast before a test.

Practice Book
Lead the Way

© Harcourt

Name _____

▶ **Underline the verb. Tell what kind of verb it is. Write** *action*
or *linking.*

1. Citizens say the Pledge of Allegiance. _____

2. "I pledge allegiance to the flag." _____

3. The Pledge is an oath of loyalty. _____

4. It promises devotion to the U.S.A. _____

5. Citizens are proud of their country. _____

6. They gladly share in the ceremony. _____

7. The United States flag is overhead. _____

8. It commands everyone's attention. _____

▶ **Complete each sentence with the kind of verb**
in parentheses ( ).

9. Fatima _____
one hand on her heart. **(action)**

10. She _____ very
happy today. **(linking)**

11. Mr. Kao _____
at his new flag. (action)

12. He _____
now a United States citizen.
(linking)

TRY THIS! Write two sentences about what it means to you to live in this country.
Use an action verb and a linking verb in your sentences.

© Harcourt

Name _____

HOMEWORK
Saguaro
Cactus

Elements of
Nonfiction
TEST PREP

▶ **Read the paragraph. Then circle the letter of the best answer to each question.**

Deserts do not have to be hot—they only have to be dry. Any area of land that gets less than ten inches of precipitation a year is classified as a desert. *Precipitation* is any form of water that falls to Earth. Rain, snow, sleet, and hail are kinds of precipitation. Some deserts are very cold. Two of these cold deserts are at the North Pole and the South Pole. Parts of the polar regions have a lot of water, but it is frozen all year long. Frozen water is not much help to plants and animals. Some of the Antarctic region is so cold that there is very little precipitation.

1 This paragraph is an example of _____.

   A fiction
   B expository nonfiction
   C science fiction
   D persuasive nonfiction

💡 **Tip**
Does the paragraph tell a story, give information, or try to make you think a certain way?

2 The purpose of this paragraph is to _____.

   F explain that some deserts are cold
   G explain rain, snow, sleet, and hail
   H describe desert plants and animals
   J show what it is like to live in the desert

💡 **Tip**
What is the main idea of the paragraph?

3 How is this paragraph organized?

   A by sequence
   B by least to most important information
   C by a main idea followed by details
   D by comparison and contrast

💡 **Tip**
Read the paragraph again. What is the relationship among the sentences?

© Harcourt

🚚 **SCHOOL-HOME CONNECTION** With your child, find examples of nonfiction writing, such as newspapers, magazines, and books. Discuss what makes them nonfiction.

Practice Book
Lead the Way

Name _____

▶ **Rewrite these sentences by using the correct present-tense form of the verb in parentheses ( ).**

1. Caleb and Mariko **(go, goes)** camping with their class.

_____

2. Mariko **(see, sees)** a wolf spider.

_____

3. Caleb **(jumps, jumped)** when he sees it.

_____

4. They **(tell, tells)** the rest of the class about the spider.

_____

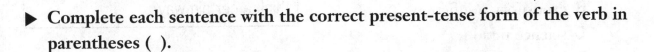

▶ **Complete each sentence with the correct present-tense form of the verb in parentheses ( ).**

5. Yasmine _____ an empty bird's nest. **(find)**

6. "This _____ like a robin's nest," she says. **(look)**

7. Zachary _____ it is a sparrow's nest. **(think)**

8. They _____ about the nest. **(argue)**

9. Yasmine _____ that they ask their teacher. **(suggest)**

10. "What kind of bird _____ a nest like this?" asks Zachary. **(make)**

11. Mr. Tam _____ them that it is a wren's nest. **(tell)**

12. Yasmine and Zachary _____ for more nests together. **(search)**

TRY THIS! Using only present-tense verbs, write a paragraph describing what you might see on a walk in the desert. Then rewrite the paragraph, using the plural subject *we*.

Name _____

Skill Reminder Some words end with an unaccented syllable pronounced /ən/. The /ən/ sound can be spelled *on*, *en*, or *an*.

▶ Fold the paper along the dotted line. As each spelling word is read aloud, write it in the blank. Then unfold your paper, and check your work. Practice any spelling words you missed.

1. _____

2. _____

3. _____

4. _____

5. _____

6. _____

7. _____

8. _____

9. _____

10. _____

11. _____

12. _____

13. _____

14. _____

15. _____

16. _____

17. _____

18. _____

19. _____

20. _____

SPELLING WORDS

1. pollen
2. even
3. urban
4. seven
5. kitchen
6. reason
7. human
8. season
9. burden
10. wagon
11. oven
12. dragon
13. horizon
14. orphan
15. sudden
16. eleven
17. button
18. canyon
19. slogan
20. golden

© Harcourt

103

Practice Book
Lead the Way

Name _____

▶ **Write the Vocabulary Word that can replace each
underlined word.**

sulkily	indifferent	protruded	loathe
undoubtedly	heartily	certainty	

I no longer felt <u>disinterested</u> **(1)** _____ about starting

school. I felt with <u>sureness</u> **(2)** _____ that I was

going to <u>hate</u> **(3)** _____ it. I frowned <u>angrily</u>

(4) _____ all the way there on my first day. But Miss

Peterson was so nice! She greeted me <u>in a warm and friendly way</u>

(5) _____ . She is <u>surely</u> **(6)** _____

the best teacher in the whole school. The pouting lower lip that <u>pushed out</u>

(7) _____ from my face curved into a smile!

▶ **Use each pair of words in one sentence.**

8. indifferent   heartily

_____

_____

9. sulkily   loathe

_____

_____

10. undoubtedly   indifferent

_____

 **TRY
THIS!** Write about the first day of a new school year. Tell what happened and how
you felt about it. Use two Vocabulary Words.

Practice Book
Lead the Way

© Harcourt

Name _____

Skill Reminder author's purpose = to entertain, to inform, or to persuade

▶ **Read the paragraphs. Then circle the letter of the best answer to each question.**

Rafael's Paragraph

The horned toad is an animal that you should never touch. It looks scary, with horns on its head and sharp spines all over its body. When it looks at someone who has disturbed it, it has a mean glare. If you see a horned toad, leave it alone!

Reina's Paragraph

The horned toad is a harmless creature that is often misunderstood. It may look scary because of its sharp spines, but it actually does no harm. The spines are just to protect it from enemies. Even though it has a mean glare, the horned toad does not hurt people at all.

1 What is the main purpose of Rafael's paragraph?

A to entertain   C to persuade
B to inform   D to give instructions

> **Tip**
> First eliminate the choices you know are wrong.

2 What is Reina's main purpose for writing her paragraph?

F to entertain   H to persuade
G to inform   J to give instructions

> **Tip**
> An author may have more than one purpose. Choose the <u>main</u> purpose.

3 Which of these is a good title for Rafael's paragraph?

A Having Fun with Horned Toads
B You Should Have a Horned Toad
C Things to Know About Horned Toads
D You Should Avoid Horned Toads

> **Tip**
> A paragraph's title should reflect the author's purpose.

© Harcourt

SCHOOL-HOME CONNECTION Talk with your child about small animals, such as squirrels, birds, and spiders, that you see where you live. Have your child write a paragraph about one of these animals. Have your child choose a purpose for this paragraph, such as to entertain, to inform, or to persuade.

Practice Book
Lead the Way

Name _____

▶ **Read the definitions. Write the meaning of each underlined word as it is used in each sentence.**

bee: (a) a type of insect; **(b)** a gathering of people
board: (a) a thin slab of material; **(b)** a group of people who direct something
pens: (a) small fenced areas for animals;
   (b) tools for writing
stories: (a) tales; **(b)** floors of a building
yard: (a) a measurement of 36 inches; **(b)** the ground next to a building

1. The building was three <u>stories</u> tall. _____

2. Her desk was only about one <u>yard</u> away from the teacher's desk.

_____

3. A <u>bee</u> flew in through the window.

_____

4. The teacher read <u>stories</u> about faraway places. _____

5. Ink and <u>pens</u> were not allowed, so Aunt Margaret wrote with a pencil.

_____

6. She also liked to write and draw on the <u>board</u>.

_____

7. The school <u>board</u> placed a United States flag in every classroom.

_____

8. Aunt Margaret's class always had a spelling <u>bee</u> on Friday.

_____

9. At recess the students played in the grassy <u>yard</u> behind the school.

_____

10. The farmer kept the pigs in <u>pens</u>.

_____

Practice Book
Lead the Way

© Harcourt

Name _____

▶ **Write the verb from each sentence in the column where it belongs.**

1. The migrant workers picked cotton all week.

2. Later they will help with the berry crop.

3. Some of the workers arrived from up North.

4. Others stayed out West most of the year.

5. A few workers will soon become landowners.

6. Many will return to the fields next year.

Past-Tense Verbs	Future-Tense Verbs

▶ **Complete each sentence with the correct form of the verb in parentheses ( ).**

7. We _____ in the middle of the year. (**move—past tense**)

8. In this town, school _____ very early. (**start—past tense**)

9. We _____ other migrant workers' children. (**meet—future tense**)

10. As we get to know each other, we _____ friends. (**become—future tense**)

TRY THIS! Think of two action verbs that end in *-ed* in the past tense. Use each verb in a past-tense sentence and in a future-tense sentence.

© Harcourt

Name _____

Skill Reminder   When you add **-ed** or **-ing** to some root words, no spelling change is needed. If the root word ends with e, drop the e before adding **-ed** or **-ing**. If the word ends with a short vowel and a consonant, double the final consonant before adding **-ed** or **-ing**.

▶ Fold the paper along the dotted line. As each spelling word is read aloud, write it in the blank. Then unfold your paper, and check your work. Practice any spelling words you missed.

1. _____
2. _____
3. _____
4. _____
5. _____
6. _____
7. _____
8. _____
9. _____
10. _____
11. _____
12. _____
13. _____
14. _____
15. _____
16. _____
17. _____
18. _____
19. _____
20. _____

SPELLING WORDS

1. stepped
2. entered
3. reaching
4. allowing
5. argued
6. speaking
7. reading
8. unfolding
9. finished
10. closing
11. hugged
12. belonged
13. divided
14. determined
15. rewarding
16. occurred
17. controlled
18. injured
19. permitting
20. practicing

© Harcourt

Practice Book
Lead the Way

Name _____

▶ **Write the Vocabulary Word that best completes each sentence.**

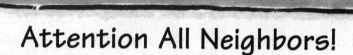

culture   chile   barbecue   mesquite   confetti   accordion

Attention All Neighbors!

This weekend we will hold an outdoor party to celebrate the

(1) _____ of the southwest. All kinds of

food will be served, including Carrie's famous salsa flavored with

spicy **(2)** _____. Ignacio will prepare

the **(3)** _____, using chips of

(4) _____. Bring your appetites!

A musician will play the **(5)** _____.

Sing along! Throw **(6)** _____!

▶ **Write the Vocabulary Word that best completes each analogy.**

7. *Sour* is to *lemon* as *spicy* is to _____.

8. *Strum* is to *guitar* as *squeeze* is to _____.

9. *Log* is to *wood chips* as *paper* is to _____.

10. *Bake* is to *oven* as *grill* is to _____.

TRY THIS! Write a paragraph about your favorite family tradition. Use at least two of the Vocabulary Words.

© Harcourt

109

Name _____

Skill Reminder **Look for time-order words to give you clues about the order in which events happen.**

▶ **Read the story. Then circle the letter of the best answer to each question.**

Every summer our neighborhood holds a giant yard sale. First, we put an ad in our town newspaper. Then, everyone meets to discuss the sale. After we make decisions about important things, like whose yard we will use and who will collect the money from customers, we talk about refreshments. During the week we put price tags on the items we want to sell. The night before the sale, we stay up late pricing last-minute items and laying everything out on tables or on the ground. Then we are ready for our customers!

1 What do the neighbors do first?

A collect money from customers

B put price tags on items

C put an ad in the paper

D lay everything out

> 💡 **Tip**
> Look for the sequence word *first*.

2 When do the neighbors discuss refreshments?

F after they make important decisions

G during the week

H the night before

J all year long

> 💡 **Tip**
> Arrange answer choices in the correct sequence.

3 Which of the following is NOT a sequence word in the paragraph?

A during

B before

C then

D meet

> 💡 **Tip**
> Which of the answer choices does not signal the order of events?

SCHOOL-HOME CONNECTION Discuss customs associated with special family celebrations. Help your child choose appropriate sequence words to explain the order of steps or events.

110

Practice Book
Lead the Way

© Harcourt

Name _____

▶ **Complete the chart with the correct form of each verb.**

Verb	Present	Past	Past with Helping Verb
1. be	am, is, are		(have, has, had)
2. go	go, goes		(have, has, had)
3. think	think, thinks		(have, has, had)
4. know	know, knows		(have, has, had)
5. wear	wear, wears		(have, has, had)

▶ **Complete each sentence with the correct past-tense form of the verb in parentheses ( ).**

6. Grandma _____ a colorful apron. **(wear)**

7. She _____ four eggs into a bowl. **(break)**

8. Then she _____ the shells in the trash. **(throw)**

9. Outside, the day had _____. **(begin)**

10. Grandpa _____ in the newspaper. **(bring)**

TRY THIS!

Write three sentences about your family, using irregular verbs.

© Harcourt

Skill Reminder   In some words, *b* and *t* are "silent."

▶ Fold the paper along the dotted line. As each spelling word is read aloud, write it in the blank. Then unfold your paper, and check your work. Practice any spelling words you missed.

1. _____
2. _____
3. _____
4. _____
5. _____
6. _____
7. _____
8. _____
9. _____
10. _____
11. _____
12. _____
13. _____
14. _____
15. _____
16. _____
17. _____
18. _____
19. _____
20. _____

SPELLING WORDS

1. lamb
2. often
3. castle
4. listen
5. comb
6. climbed
7. fasten
8. crumbs
9. soften
10. thumb
11. doubt
12. whistle
13. honest
14. rhyme
15. answer
16. column
17. numb
18. tomb
19. glisten
20. hasten

Practice Book
Lead the Way

© Harcourt

▶ **Read the following paragraphs. Then complete the outline below.**

The history of gold dates back thousands of years. Experts believe that early humans probably used gold as a tool. By 5,000 years ago, the ancient Egyptians had learned to work gold into beautiful jewelry and carved statues. In China, people began using gold squares as money about 3,000 years ago.

In the United States, people first discovered gold in North Carolina in 1803. For more than twenty-five years, North Carolina supplied the country with all its gold for gold coins.

People still mine gold in the United States. However, most of the gold close to Earth's surface is gone. Now scientists study photographs of Earth taken from space satellites, looking for signs of buried gold. Then they dig pits or underground mines to find rocks that hold the precious gold.

Gold

I. People have used gold for thousands of years

    A. _____

    B. _____

    C. _____

II. _____

    A. Gold discovered in North Carolina in 1803

    B. _____

III. Mining in the United States today

    A. _____

    B. Gold at Earth's surface is gone

        1. _____

        2. _____

SCHOOL-HOME CONNECTION With your child, watch a television show about a science or history topic. Have your child make a brief outline as you watch the show.

115

Practice Book
Lead the Way

Name _____

▶ **Write the contraction for each word pair.**

1. she is _____

2. have not _____

3. would not _____

4. is not _____

5. I have _____

6. he had _____

7. it is _____

8. do not _____

▶ **Write the negative from each sentence.**

9. Nobody earns a living panning for gold today. _____

10. Panning for gold was never a sure way to earn money. _____

▶ **Rewrite each sentence. Get rid of double negatives. Use the
correct pronoun or contraction.**

11. You never wanted to be no miner.

_____

12. Your sure its too hard a life?

_____

**TRY
THIS!** Use each word group in a sentence: *its/it's* and *their/they're/there*.
Use each word in a sentence: *nobody* and *never*.

© Harcourt

Name _____

▶ **Underline the verb. Circle the adverb that describes it. Then write whether the adverb tells *where, when,* or *how*.**

1. The huge ox rushed over. _____

2. It quickly drank from the trough. _____

3. The pioneer shouted loudly. _____

4. He never saw such a thirsty beast. _____

5. A few horses stood nearby. _____

6. Now the ox felt content. _____

7. It lay down with a grunt. _____

8. Later, the pioneer brought the wagon. _____

9. Preparing the wagon, he whistled happily. _____

10. The ox snorted angrily. _____

▶ **Rewrite each sentence. Add an adverb that gives the information in parentheses ( ).**

11. The ox took a nap. (when)

   _____

   _____

12. The pioneers rested. (where)

   _____

   _____

 TRY THIS! Draw three pictures of people you know. Then write captions for your drawings, using adverbs in each sentence. For example: *Grandma smiles happily.*

© Harcourt

Skill Reminder Homophones are words that sound alike but are spelled differently and have different meanings.

▶ Fold the paper along the dotted line. As each spelling word is read aloud, write it in the blank. Then unfold your paper, and check your work. Practice any spelling words you missed.

1. _____
2. _____
3. _____
4. _____
5. _____
6. _____
7. _____
8. _____
9. _____
10. _____
11. _____
12. _____
13. _____
14. _____
15. _____
16. _____
17. _____
18. _____
19. _____
20. _____

SPELLING WORDS

1. some
2. sum
3. tale
4. tail
5. close
6. clothes
7. piece
8. peace
9. plains
10. planes
11. blue
12. blew
13. night
14. knight
15. peddle
16. pedal
17. sight
18. site
19. stake
20. steak

© Harcourt

Name _____

▶ **Write the Vocabulary Word that best completes each sentence.**

bellowing   softhearted   ration   tragedy   fateful   gadgets

Many tall tales tell of legendary characters who are big both in size and in deeds. Somehow though, we tend to think of giants as unpleasant. Remember the giant in "Jack and the Beanstalk?" Was he

kind and **(1)** _____, or was he mean and scary? If the giant had plenty of food, do you think he would share it freely

with others or **(2)** _____ it in very small amounts?

Can you picture the size of his household **(3)** _____, such as his can opener or nutcracker? It is a

(4) _____ that because of one mean giant, other giants are thought of in the same way. You would never hear Paul Bunyan

(5) _____ at his pet ox unless he thought Babe was

lost. He was the best logger ever. It was a **(6)** _____ day when Paul Bunyan decided to stop working.

▶ **Write the Vocabulary Word that means the *opposite* of each word below.**

7. comedy   _____

8. strict   _____

9. whispering   _____

TRY THIS! Make up your own story about something unusual that Paul Bunyan and Babe did. Use at least two Vocabulary Words.

Practice Book
Lead the Way

© Harcourt

Name _____

Skill Reminder	fact = can be supported by evidence

opinion = expresses a belief, a judgment, or a feeling

▶ **Read the paragraph. Then circle the letter of the best answer to each question.**

Many tall tales are about real people, such as Johnny Appleseed and Davy Crockett. My favorite tall tales are about Paul Bunyan, a fictional character. There are many stories about his adventures with his friend Babe the Blue Ox. My sister says that the stories are silly. She says that an ox can't be blue. I don't care what she thinks. These famous American stories are fun to read and reread. One of the funniest stories is about the bees and the mosquitoes. Paul thought he was solving a problem, but he only made things worse.

1 Which sentence from the paragraph states a fact?

A Many tall tales are about real people, such as Johnny Appleseed and Davy Crockett.

B My favorite tall tales are about Paul Bunyan, a fictional character.

C These famous American stories are fun to read and reread.

D One of the funniest stories is about the bees and the mosquitoes.

💡 **Tip**
Eliminate statements that are clearly opinions.

2 Which part of *These famous American stories are fun to read and reread* tells you that it is an opinion?

F These famous

G American stories

H are fun

J to read and reread

💡 **Tip**
Descriptive adjectives often reveal an author's opinion.

3 Which statement is an opinion?

A There are many stories about Paul's adventures with his friend Babe the Blue Ox.

B Paul thought he was solving a problem, but he only made things worse.

C Many tall tales are about real people.

D The stories are silly.

💡 **Tip**
A statement about a fictional character can still be a fact.

SCHOOL-HOME CONNECTION With your child, take turns stating facts about objects you see in your home. Then take turns stating opinions about those objects.

124

Practice Book
Lead the Way

© Harcourt

Name _____

▶ **Rewrite each sentence, using the correct form of the adverb in parentheses ( ).**

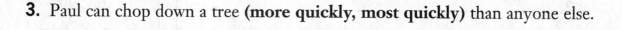

1. Babe grew **(taller, tallest)** than a barn.

   _____

2. Paul Bunyan works the **(harder, hardest)** of all the loggers.

   _____

3. Paul can chop down a tree **(more quickly, most quickly)** than anyone else.

   _____

4. Loggers eat the **(more hungrily, most hungrily)** of all the people in the world.

   _____

5. Paul can laugh **(louder, loudest)** than a clap of thunder.

   _____

▶ **Complete each sentence with the correct form of the adverb in parentheses ( ).**

6. The wind blew _____ than a tornado. **(strongly)**

7. The Mississippi flowed _____ of all the rivers. **(fast)**

8. The bird soared _____ than the clouds. **(high)**

9. Of all the insects, the mosquitoes attacked the

   _____. **(fiercely)**

10. The rain fell _____ in the valley than in the mountains. **(heavily)**

Practice Book
Lead the Way

© Harcourt

Name _____

Skill Reminder   In a VCCV word, the first syllable usually has
a short vowel sound. The word is divided into syllables
between the two consonants.

▶ Fold the paper along the dotted line. As each
spelling word is read aloud, write it in the blank.
Then unfold your paper, and check your work.
Practice any spelling words you missed.

1. _____

2. _____

3. _____

4. _____

5. _____

6. _____

7. _____

8. _____

9. _____

10. _____

11. _____

12. _____

13. _____

14. _____

15. _____

16. _____

17. _____

18. _____

19. _____

20. _____

SPELLING WORDS

1. practice
2. members
3. dinner
4. suppose
5. except
6. problem
7. shallow
8. stubborn
9. logger
10. cotton
11. object
12. shelter
13. distance
14. pattern
15. captive
16. publish
17. sitting
18. tractor
19. servant
20. hidden

© Harcourt

Practice Book
Lead the Way

Name _____

▶ **Write the Vocabulary Word that fits best with each pair.
One word will be used twice.**

| carnivorous | boggiest | chemicals | dissolve |
| accidentally | fertilizer | victim | |

1. melt
   liquid

   _____

2. grow
   plants

   _____

3. meat-eating
   hungry

   _____

4. unintentionally
   unplanned

   _____

5. swampy
   soggy

   _____

6. not on purpose
   unexpectedly

   _____

7. injured
   harmed

   _____

8. scientist
   substances

   _____

▶ **Write the Vocabulary Word that means the
opposite of each term below.**

9. vegetable-eating _____

10. solidify _____

11. attacker _____

12. intentionally _____

TRY THIS! Imagine that you are a plant or an animal. Write sentences that tell what you do to survive the dangers where you live. Use some Vocabulary Words.

© Harcourt

Practice Book
Lead the Way

Name _____

Skill Reminder related words = words with the same root that have related meanings

▶ **Read the paragraph. Then circle the letter of the best answer to each question.**

This year, my school is going to start a school garden. The students of each grade will have a part of the garden to plant with anything they want. Most of the *youngsters* in first grade want to plant flowers. The older kids plan to have vegetables in their section. The students in my grade have a *superb* idea. We are going to plant unusual plants that will surprise all the students in the other grades. I can *envision* how the garden will look when our spiderworts, beebalm, and butterfly bushes grow.

1 Which word is related to the word *youngsters*?
   A your
   B youngest
   C yogurt
   D yonder

💡 **Tip**
Which answer choice shares the same root word as the word *youngsters*?

2 Which word is related to the word *superb*?
   F soup
   G spur
   H supper
   J superior

💡 **Tip**
Find the answer choice that belongs to the same word family as the word *superb*.

3 Which phrase means the same as the word *envision*?
   A to see in your mind
   B to follow someone
   C to remember
   D to create something

💡 **Tip**
Think of other words you know that have the word root *vis*. Which answer choice has a related meaning?

© Harcourt

SCHOOL-HOME CONNECTION With your child, make a list of words that have the root word *graph*. Talk about how the meanings of these words are related.

128

Practice Book
Lead the Way

▶ **Underline the preposition. Circle the object of the preposition.**

1. The flytrap grew tall in a tiny pot.

2. It leaned into the sunshine.

3. For a while, it rested quietly.

4. A small fly buzzed over the plant.

5. After a few minutes, the trap snapped.

6. The buzzing of the small insect stopped.

▶ **Use a preposition from the box to complete each sentence. Use each word only once. Use capital letters when necessary.**

across	with	from	into	before	of

7. _____ noon, the flytrap ate seven bugs.

8. The bugs fell _____ its trap and dissolved.

9. The leaves were armed _____ trigger hairs.

10. The tiniest insects were safe _____ the trap.

11. They walked _____ the hairs unharmed.

12. Many _____ the flytraps' habitats have been destroyed.

TRY THIS! Choose three of the prepositions from the box above. Use each of them in a separate sentence about plants.

Name _____

Skill Reminder   Many two-syllable words contain the VCV pattern. In these words, the first syllable often has a long vowel sound.

▶ Fold the paper along the dotted line. As each spelling word is read aloud, write it in the blank. Then unfold your paper, and check your work. Practice any spelling words you missed.

1. _____
2. _____
3. _____
4. _____
5. _____
6. _____
7. _____
8. _____
9. _____
10. _____
11. _____
12. _____
13. _____
14. _____
15. _____
16. _____
17. _____
18. _____
19. _____
20. _____

SPELLING WORDS

1. major
2. cedar
3. spiders
4. locate
5. ruler
6. motive
7. raven
8. pilot
9. silent
10. super
11. paper
12. native
13. rivals
14. solar
15. bison
16. legal
17. humor
18. moment
19. nature
20. virus

Practice Book
Lead the Way

Name _____

▶ **Write Vocabulary Words to complete the letter.**

transformed	investigate	enthusiastically
decor	apparently	corridor

Dear Cousin,

The **(1)** _____ in our classroom has changed

since your last visit. My friends and I **(2)** _____

the room into a tropical rain forest! It looks so cool! You don't suspect

anything when you're outside in the **(3)** _____.

But when you walk into the room, wow! I've never written so

(4) _____ about a class project before!

The city newspaper is **(5)** _____ going to have

a story about it. I will **(6)** _____ this further

and let you know for sure.

Your cousin,
Aldo

▶ **Write the Vocabulary Word that is a synonym for each word below.**

7. energetically _____

8. research _____

9. seemingly _____

10. changed _____

 TRY THIS! Think of a way you'd like to decorate your classroom or a room at home.
Use at least three Vocabulary Words in your description.

© Harcourt

Practice Book
Lead the Way

Name _____

Skill Reminder   author's purpose = to entertain, to inform, or to persuade

▶ **Read the passage. Then circle the letter of the best answer to each question.**

Jungle Outfitters

We lead the safest, most exciting trips into the Amazon rain forest and have the lowest prices! Come join us for three weeks of adventure and fun.

Our guides are the most experienced you can find. Take this chance to find out what secrets the rain forest holds.

Travel with us deep into the rain forest! Enjoy our canoes and the beauty of this wonderful region!

Call today to find out what's in store for you in the Amazon rain forest.

1 What purpose does the author have for writing this passage?

  A to entertain
  B to inform
  C to persuade
  D to ask questions

💡 **Tip**
Examine the structure of the passage and the title.

2 Why did the author of this passage choose this purpose?

  F The author wants to go on a trip to the rain forest.
  G The author works for the company that sells the rain forest trips.
  H The author has studied rain forests.
  J The author likes to tell stories about the rain forest.

💡 **Tip**
Think about what you know about advertising.

3 The author would probably agree that

  A you shouldn't go on a rain forest trip offered by another company.
  B the rain forest is a scary place.
  C there isn't much to see in the rain forest.
  D it's not important to have an experienced guide on a trip to the rain forest.

💡 **Tip**
Eliminate answer choices that are obviously wrong.

© Harcourt

SCHOOL-HOME CONNECTION Talk with your child about something that you enjoy doing together. Have your child write a paragraph about the activity, with a specific purpose in mind: to inform, to persuade, or to entertain.

132

Practice Book
Lead the Way

Name _____

▶ **Underline the prepositional phrase. Circle the preposition.**

1. Rubber plants grew in the rain forest.

2. Lucette perched on a high branch.

3. After a few minutes, she began talking.

4. She squawked at the people below.

5. A green snake with black markings appeared.

6. We almost fell into the pond.

7. We asked for a volunteer to lead us.

8. Our leader went ahead of us, and we
   formed a line.

▶ **Complete each sentence with a prepositional phrase.**

9. Bolivia brought her parrot _____.

10. _____, Lucette seemed content.

11. She preened her feathers _____.

12. She climbed _____ very carefully.

13. The students _____ clapped.

14. The green parrot then swooped _____.

15. _____ some students left.

16. Then Bolivia walked _____.

TRY THIS! Rewrite this sentence three times: *The students saw a parrot.*
Add a different prepositional phrase each time. How does the sentence's
meaning change?

Skill Reminder **A longer word can be divided into syllables to make it easier to spell. Knowing spelling rules for consonant-vowel patterns (such as VCCV and VCV) will help you when spelling longer words.**

▶ Fold the paper along the dotted line. As each spelling word is read aloud, write it in the blank. Then unfold your paper, and check your work. Practice any spelling words you missed.

1. _____
2. _____
3. _____
4. _____
5. _____
6. _____
7. _____
8. _____
9. _____
10. _____
11. _____
12. _____
13. _____
14. _____
15. _____
16. _____
17. _____
18. _____
19. _____
20. _____

SPELLING WORDS

1. difficult
2. probably
3. beginning
4. direction
5. discover
6. excellent
7. important
8. imagine
9. energy
10. remember
11. different
12. another
13. beautiful
14. dangerous
15. government
16. interest
17. becoming
18. description
19. engineer
20. wonderful

© Harcourt

Skills and Strategies Index

Skills and Strategies Index

SPELLING

RESEARCH AND INFORMATION SKILLS

VOCABULARY

End-of-Selection Tests

Grade 4

The Gardener

Directions: For items 1–18, fill in the circle in front of the correct answer. For items 19–20, write the answer.

Vocabulary

1. Megan was _____ to get to school because she was going on a class trip.
   - (A) vacant
   - (B) anxious
   - (C) adore
   - (D) retire

2. Todd has on a bright red shirt, so you will have no trouble _____ him.
   - (A) sprucing
   - (B) anxious
   - (C) recognizing
   - (D) adore

3. My baseball team cleaned up a _____ lot so we could make a ball field.
   - (A) retire
   - (B) sprucing
   - (C) vacant
   - (D) recognizing

4. All the children _____ the baby kittens because they are so cute and loving.
   - (A) adore
   - (B) retire
   - (C) sprucing
   - (D) vacant

5. They spent a lot of time _____ up their house because it needed a lot of repairs.
   - (A) sprucing
   - (B) adore
   - (C) recognizing
   - (D) retire

© Harcourt

6. My grandfather can't wait to _____ from his job so he can travel around the world.

Ⓐ retire   Ⓑ adore

Ⓒ sprucing   Ⓓ anxious

Comprehension

7. Why does Lydia go to live with Uncle Jim?

Ⓐ because her parents want her to go to school in the city

Ⓑ because she wants to learn how to bake

Ⓒ because she wants to plant flowers

Ⓓ because Uncle Jim is helping out until her father gets work

8. Why does Lydia Grace write to Uncle Jim the first time?

Ⓐ Her mother tells her to write to him.

Ⓑ Uncle Jim had chased her mother up trees when they were little.

Ⓒ She wants him to know she will be helpful to him when she comes to live with him.

Ⓓ Uncle Jim loves to get letters.

9. Why does Lydia feel that she can help Uncle Jim?

Ⓐ because she is his niece

Ⓑ because she is small but strong

Ⓒ because she is anxious to learn baking

Ⓓ because she knows a lot about gardening

10. What excites Lydia when she arrives at Uncle Jim's?

Ⓐ seeds and bulbs   Ⓑ a garden and a sidewalk

Ⓒ window boxes and sunshine   Ⓓ a pretty dress and a hat

© Harcourt

Practice Book
Lead the Way

11. What does Lydia Grace notice about Uncle Jim?

(A) He doesn't talk.

(B) He doesn't smile.

(C) He loves drawings.

(D) He has a big nose and mustache.

12. Lydia Grace thinks Uncle Jim likes the poem she wrote because he _____ .

(A) reads it aloud and puts it in his pocket

(B) says that he likes it

(C) smiles but says nothing about it

(D) smiles

13. Lydia Grace remembers Grandma's saying, "April showers bring May flowers." In this selection, *April showers bring May flowers* means _____ .

(A) it rains only in April   (B) flowers need water to grow

(C) all flowers bloom in May   (D) seeds are sprouting in April

14. Where is Lydia Grace's secret place?

(A) on the farm   (B) in her bedroom

(C) in the vacant lot   (D) on the roof

15. What does Lydia Grace want most to happen at the bakery?

(A) to keep Otis for her own

(B) to be helpful

(C) to see Uncle Jim smile

(D) to be able to knead dough well

16. What challenge does Lydia Grace face in this selection?

(A) learning how to speak Latin   (B) living away from home

(C) finding a secret place   (D) taking care of Otis

© Harcourt

17. Which best describes Lydia Grace?

Ⓐ cheerful   Ⓑ nervous

Ⓒ lazy   Ⓓ lonely

18. Why does Lydia Grace use capital letters to write the words "I'M COMING HOME!"?

Ⓐ She likes capital letters.

Ⓑ She makes a mistake.

Ⓒ She is excited to be going home.

Ⓓ Ed and Emma tell her to use capital letters.

19. What trick does Lydia Grace play on Uncle Jim?

_____

_____

_____

_____

_____

20. When Lydia Grace says "I truly believe that cake equals one thousand smiles," what does she mean?

_____

_____

_____

_____

_____

© Harcourt

Amelia and Eleanor Go for a Ride

Directions: For items 1–18, fill in the circle in front of the correct answer. For items 19–20, write the answer.

Vocabulary

1. Danny knew it wasn't _____ to buy a new car when there was nothing wrong with his old one.

  Ⓐ practical　　　　　　Ⓑ outspoken
  Ⓒ elegant　　　　　　Ⓓ starstruck

2. Heather took her dog for a _____ walk each day.

  Ⓐ elegant　　　　　　Ⓑ elevations
  Ⓒ brisk　　　　　　　Ⓓ practical

3. Maria is very _____ about things that are important to her.

  Ⓐ marveled　　　　　Ⓑ miniatures
  Ⓒ elevations　　　　　Ⓓ outspoken

4. We could see the different _____ of the mountains from the window of the airplane.

  Ⓐ starstruck　　　　　Ⓑ brisk
  Ⓒ elevations　　　　　Ⓓ salary

5. Aunt Sophie has a collection of over fifty _____ on one shelf.

  Ⓐ elevations　　　　　Ⓑ miniatures
  Ⓒ immigrants　　　　　Ⓓ starstruck

6. Getting dressed up made Jenna feel _____ .

  Ⓐ elegant　　　　　　Ⓑ practical
  Ⓒ modest　　　　　　Ⓓ marveled

7. The darkness helped me see the beauty of the _____ sky.

  Ⓐ elevations　　　　　Ⓑ outspoken
  Ⓒ miniatures　　　　　Ⓓ starstruck

8. The teacher _____ at the fact that every student earned an A on the spelling test.

(A) outspoken   (B) marveled

(C) practical   (D) starstruck

Comprehension

9. In this selection, what does the expression "birds of a feather" say about Amelia and Eleanor?

(A) They were alike in many ways.

(B) They had nothing in common.

(C) They both loved birds.

(D) They wished they could fly like real birds.

10. Amelia and Eleanor are both famous. They are _____ .

(A) a pilot and the wife of a president

(B) a president and a singer

(C) a television star and an inventor

(D) an actress and a reporter

11. What is so unusual about Amelia flying an airplane in 1933?

(A) Airplanes hadn't been invented yet.

(B) Amelia hated airplanes.

(C) Her husband wouldn't let her fly.

(D) Very few women were flying airplanes back then.

12. Why does Amelia encourage Eleanor to get her student pilot's license?

(A) Amelia knows Eleanor can do anything she sets her mind to.

(B) Amelia wants Eleanor to take her place as a pilot.

(C) Amelia knows Eleanor's husband wants her to fly.

(D) Eleanor asks Amelia to get the license for her.

13. Why does everyone at the dinner party want to know what it is like to fly at night?

Ⓐ They don't have anything else to talk about.

Ⓑ They don't believe that anyone has flown at night.

Ⓒ They want to make Amelia feel important.

Ⓓ Very few people have ever flown at night and they are curious.

14. Amelia and Eleanor are similar because they both are _____ .

Ⓐ very timid individuals

Ⓑ very adventurous

Ⓒ married to famous husbands

Ⓓ afraid of night flying

15. What does Amelia ask Eleanor to do after dinner that is surprising?

Ⓐ have more dessert

Ⓑ take a flight to Baltimore so she can see the night sky

Ⓒ have lunch the next day

Ⓓ go shopping with her

16. Why does Eleanor say it is like sitting on top of the world when they are flying?

Ⓐ They are so high up, the buildings look like tiny miniatures.

Ⓑ They are at the top of a tall mountain.

Ⓒ They go around the world.

Ⓓ They are flying very fast.

17. Why does the reporter ask Eleanor if she felt "safe knowing a girl was flying that ship"?

Ⓐ People think it is strange that a woman can fly a plane.

Ⓑ The reporter can't think of anything else to ask.

Ⓒ Eleanor looked scared when she got off the plane.

Ⓓ Amelia is not a good pilot.

18. Instead of going into the White House, Amelia and Eleanor
go _____ .

Ⓐ to the Secret Service agent's home

Ⓑ back to the airport

Ⓒ for a ride in Eleanor's brand-new car

Ⓓ to the movies

19. The author chooses to write about Amelia and Eleanor's friendship
because

_____

_____

_____

_____

_____

_____

_____

20. Why do Amelia and Eleanor become such good friends?

_____

_____

_____

_____

_____

_____

© Harcourt

The Garden of Happiness

Directions: For items 1–18, fill in the circle in front of the correct answer. For items 19–20, write the answer.

Vocabulary

1. Our car _____ on the ice, but luckily, we were able to stop safely.
Ⓐ mural   Ⓑ skidded
Ⓒ haze   Ⓓ inhaled

2. I _____ deeply when my mother took a freshly baked loaf of bread from the oven.
Ⓐ haze   Ⓑ inhaled
Ⓒ venture   Ⓓ lavender

3. The color _____ is a light shade of purple.
Ⓐ mural   Ⓑ yellow
Ⓒ red   Ⓓ lavender

4. The _____ that filled the sky made it hard to see the mountains.
Ⓐ haze   Ⓑ lavender
Ⓒ mural   Ⓓ burrows

5. In our city, each school painted a _____ on the side of a tall building.
Ⓐ lavender   Ⓑ skidded
Ⓒ mural   Ⓓ inhaled

Comprehension

6. Most of the story takes place in _____.
Ⓐ an empty lot   Ⓑ a garage
Ⓒ an apartment building Ⓓ Marisol's home

© Harcourt

Practice Book
Lead the Way

7. Neighbors on Marisol's block clear an empty lot so they can _____ .
   - (A) meet there
   - (B) have a party
   - (C) have a street festival
   - (D) plant a garden

8. Why can't Marisol have a garden plot like the other people have?
   - (A) All the land is divided up.
   - (B) She does not know what to plant.
   - (C) Teenagers are painting a mural.
   - (D) She didn't help clean up the empty lot.

9. How does Marisol feel when she finds a patch of soil for her garden?
   - (A) disappointed because it is so small
   - (B) very happy to have a little space for herself
   - (C) annoyed that she cannot have a larger plot
   - (D) no longer interested in having a garden

10. What problem does Marisol have with her garden?
    - (A) She has to learn how to plant things.
    - (B) She is working with a very small patch of soil.
    - (C) She needs to find something to plant.
    - (D) She can't find time to look after her garden.

11. What problem does Marisol share with the teenagers?
    - (A) None of them knew exactly what to do with their project.
    - (B) No one had money to buy what they needed for their projects.
    - (C) None of them liked planting gardens.
    - (D) They mostly wanted to play and not work.

12. To solve her problem, Marisol _____ .
    - (A) asks Mrs. Rodriguez for more space
    - (B) asks Mr. Castro for one of his seedlings
    - (C) decides that the space is too small
    - (D) takes a big flat seed from the pigeons

13. Marisol often sees Mr. Ortiz in his plot, resting in a chair. In this selection, *plot* means _____ .

Ⓐ the main events in a story

Ⓑ a small piece of land in a cemetery

Ⓒ a small area planted with vegetables

Ⓓ a secret plan to accomplish something

14. For a long time, Marisol does not know _____ .

Ⓐ what the other neighbors planted

Ⓑ what kind of seed she has planted

Ⓒ how she will water her plant

Ⓓ if she is taking care of her plant the right way

15. What does Marisol learn about sunflowers?

Ⓐ Sunflowers grow in many places around the world.

Ⓑ Sunflowers are considered to be weeds.

Ⓒ The sunflower seeds taste good.

Ⓓ Sunflowers grow only in Mexico.

16. How does the sunflower affect the neighborhood?

Ⓐ It attracts bees.

Ⓑ It makes people happy.

Ⓒ Its seeds spread everywhere.

Ⓓ People keep stealing its seeds.

17. Marisol is sad toward the end of the selection because _____ .

Ⓐ she falls down in the garden and is hurt

Ⓑ her sunflower begins to wither and die

Ⓒ her friends never come back to the garden

Ⓓ she doesn't have beans or tomatoes to eat anymore

Practice Book
Lead the Way

18. Why is the garden called The Garden of Happiness?

(A) It makes everyone happy to grow and raise vegetables there.

(B) No one can be sad in such a pretty place.

(C) It is a good name for an empty lot.

(D) Everyone thinks that a happy garden name will make the vegetables grow well.

19. What does Mrs. Rodriguez explain to Marisol about the sunflower?

_____

_____

_____

_____

_____

20. Why does everyone call Marisol to the street?

_____

_____

_____

_____

_____

The Case of Pablo's Nose

Directions: For items 1–18, fill in the circle in front of the correct answer. For items 19–20, write the answer.

Vocabulary

1. Tasha could barely hear the old man as he _____ to himself.
- Ⓐ retorted
- Ⓑ sculptor
- Ⓒ muttered
- Ⓓ alibi

2. Vanessa's body was _____ every day because of her new exercise program.
- Ⓐ straightaway
- Ⓑ strengthening
- Ⓒ sculptor
- Ⓓ alibi

3. When people saw what Oliver carved out of st___e, they called him a great _____ .
- Ⓐ alibi
- Ⓑ ___ort
- Ⓒ sculptor
- Ⓓ mutter

4. Rather than wait until la___ I want you to do your chores _____ .
- Ⓐ straightaway
- Ⓑ retorted
- Ⓒ strengthen___
- Ⓓ muttered

5. When ___ woman was wrongly accused, she _____ that she was innocent.
- Ⓐ whistled
- Ⓑ sculptor
- Ⓒ straightaway
- Ⓓ retorted

6. Ben's _____ was that he had been working at home, but no one else had seen him there.
- Ⓐ alibi
- Ⓑ scholarship
- Ⓒ sculptor
- Ⓓ strengthening

Comprehension

7. When Pablo says, "My nose. It's been stolen!" he means _____ .

Ⓐ the original nose from the statue

Ⓑ a drawing of Abraham Lincoln's nose

Ⓒ Encyclopedia Brown's sculpture

Ⓓ the nose that Pablo sculpted for the contest

8. What is Pablo's first step in sculpting the new nose?

Ⓐ making a mold of the statue's face

Ⓑ mixing the stone with a special glue

Ⓒ leaving the sculpture outside to weather

Ⓓ shaping the mixture into a copy of the wax model

9. When Pablo says he thought he "had a good chance of nosing out everyone," he means that he _____ .

Ⓐ has the biggest nose in Idaville

Ⓑ has a good sense of smell

Ⓒ thinks he will win the contest

Ⓓ is the luckiest person in town

10. Pablo uses photographs of Abraham Lincoln because he _____ .

Ⓐ likes Abraham Lincoln's face

Ⓑ wants to make the nose look realistic

Ⓒ wants to be a photographer

Ⓓ doesn't know how to make a nose

11. What does Sally mean when she tells Pablo that he is "a regular plastic surgeon"?

Ⓐ He is a doctor and fixes people's noses.

Ⓑ The nose is Pablo's masterpiece.

Ⓒ The nose is not the right color or texture.

Ⓓ He works as hard as a doctor doing plastic surgery on a person.

© Harcourt

12. Why do the detectives know that Martha Katz could not have taken the nose?

Ⓐ She does not have a purple bicycle.

Ⓑ She is in Maine for the summer with her grandparents.

Ⓒ She and Joan are at camp in North Carolina.

Ⓓ She does not have a red shirt.

13. Why is Desmoana Lowry a suspect?

Ⓐ She is jealous of Pablo.

Ⓑ She owns a blue shirt.

Ⓒ She entered the nose contest.

Ⓓ She owns a purple bicycle.

14. What is Desmoana's biggest alibi?

Ⓐ She has not ridden her bicycle for nearly a year.

Ⓑ She is wearing a red shirt.

Ⓒ She was at home when the robbery took place.

Ⓓ She was at camp earlier in the day.

15. What is this story about?

Ⓐ Pablo Pizzaro, Idaville's greatest artist

Ⓑ Abraham Lincoln's nose

Ⓒ catching a thief

Ⓓ Encyclopedia Brown's detective service

16. How does Desmoana show her guilt?

Ⓐ by saying she's not interested in bikes anymore

Ⓑ by doing tricks on her bicycle

Ⓒ by hiding her bicycle behind the water heater

Ⓓ by not being good at riding a bike

Practice Book
Lead the Way

17. Why does Pablo's nose win the New Nose Now contest?

   Ⓐ He is Idaville's greatest artist.

   Ⓑ The nose is found.

   Ⓒ His nose is the only one entered in the contest.

   Ⓓ His nose is a masterpiece.

18. Which best describes Encyclopedia Brown?

   Ⓐ jumps to conclusions

   Ⓑ thinks things through carefully

   Ⓒ is not willing to try new things

   Ⓓ wants everyone to be honest

19. Why does Desmoana steal Pablo's nose?

_____

_____

_____

_____

20. What lesson can Pablo learn from this incident?

_____

_____

_____

_____

_____

© Harcourt

Practice Book
Lead the Way

Blue Willow

Directions: For items 1–18, fill in the circle in front of the correct answer. For items 19–20, write the answer.

Vocabulary

1. Grandma will _____ the way my mother decorated with purple because she hates purple.
   - Ⓐ sulkily
   - Ⓑ loathe
   - Ⓒ indifferent
   - Ⓓ undoubtedly

2. It is a real _____ that my brothers will be home on school nights.
   - Ⓐ certainty
   - Ⓑ protruded
   - Ⓒ heartily
   - Ⓓ indifferent

3. Grandpa laughed _____ at the jokes Jackson was telling him.
   - Ⓐ sulkily
   - Ⓑ indifferent
   - Ⓒ heartily
   - Ⓓ loathe

4. I replied in an _____ manner when Carrie wanted to go to a movie I had already seen.
   - Ⓐ undoubtedly
   - Ⓑ certainty
   - Ⓒ protruded
   - Ⓓ indifferent

5. I looked at my father _____ when he said I had to go to bed early.
   - Ⓐ certainty
   - Ⓑ sulkily
   - Ⓒ spiny
   - Ⓓ undoubtedly

6. Mom's apple pie is _____ the best in the world!
   - Ⓐ undoubtedly
   - Ⓑ loathe
   - Ⓒ heartily
   - Ⓓ certainty

7. No one could figure out what _____ from the roof of the building.
   - Ⓐ indifferent
   - Ⓑ habitat
   - Ⓒ protruded
   - Ⓓ loathe

Comprehension

8. At the beginning of the selection, Janey doesn't want to go to the camp school because _____ .

Ⓐ she hates school

Ⓑ she doesn't like her teacher

Ⓒ school is hard for her

Ⓓ she wants to go to the town school

9. "We'll keep with our own kind," her father had once said when Janey had remonstrated with him. In this selection, *remonstrated with* means _____ .

Ⓐ agreed   Ⓑ showed

Ⓒ pleaded against   Ⓓ tricked

10. Why won't going to the "regular" school satisfy Janey any longer?

Ⓐ She is far ahead of the students in that school.

Ⓑ She wants to really belong somewhere.

Ⓒ She agrees that she should be with her own kind.

Ⓓ Her friend, Lupe, isn't there anymore.

11. Why does Janey assume that she will not learn much in the camp school?

Ⓐ It is just a one-room school house.

Ⓑ She is not welcome there.

Ⓒ She already knows much more than the other students.

Ⓓ All the students have different educational backgrounds.

12. How does Janey know for sure that school has not yet started?

Ⓐ The flag is not flying.

Ⓑ It is too early in the day.

Ⓒ Everyone is still out in the fields.

Ⓓ There aren't any cars in the parking lot.

Practice Book
Lead the Way

13. Who goes to the camp school?

  (A) children who want to learn outdoor skills

  (B) children who sign up for summer camp

  (C) children whose parents live in the school district

  (D) children whose parents work for a short time in the cotton fields

14. Why is there a village of little houses near the cotton fields?

  (A) People need shelter from the midday heat when working in the fields.

  (B) The workers don't want to live in town.

  (C) During the picking season, workers live there.

  (D) The camps always have row upon row of houses.

15. How long will Janey probably attend this camp school?

  (A) until she has learned what she needs to know

  (B) until it is time for the cotton pickers to move on

  (C) until she is old enough to graduate

  (D) through the next two seasons of picking cotton

16. When the teacher says, "No ten-o'clock-scholar about you," what does she mean?

  (A) Janey is late for school.

  (B) Janey is early for school.

  (C) All students come at ten o'clock.

  (D) There are smart students at the camp school.

17. What convinces Janey that her teacher is all right?

  (A) The teacher quotes a passage from Mother Goose.

  (B) The teacher gets out of the dusty sedan smiling and merry.

  (C) The teacher calls Janey's new pet a horned toad.

  (D) The teacher names the horned toad Fafnir.

© Harcourt

18. Why does Janey tiptoe into the school?

    (A) Her teacher is very tall.

    (B) The floor is wet.

    (C) She is entertaining the teacher.

    (D) Janey is happy she has found a wonderful teacher.

19. How does Miss Peterson show consideration for her students?

_____

_____

_____

_____

_____

20. Why are the children able to tell their teacher so much about other parts of the United States?

_____

_____

_____

_____

_____

© Harcourt

In My Family

Directions: For items 1–18, fill in the circle in front of the correct answer. For items 19–20, write the answer.

Vocabulary

1. People threw _____ at the bride and groom after the wedding.
   - Ⓐ confetti
   - Ⓑ barbecue
   - Ⓒ culture
   - Ⓓ mesquite

2. Joe put _____ chips into the fire and then cooked some chicken on the grill.
   - Ⓐ chile
   - Ⓑ mesquite
   - Ⓒ accordion
   - Ⓓ culture

3. Our whole school had a _____ outside when the weather turned warm.
   - Ⓐ confetti
   - Ⓑ culture
   - Ⓒ protruded
   - Ⓓ barbecue

4. One of the spices that is used in some Mexican food is _____ .
   - Ⓐ chile
   - Ⓑ accordion
   - Ⓒ culture
   - Ⓓ confetti

5. Todd learned about the _____ of the country he wanted to visit.
   - Ⓐ barbecue
   - Ⓑ confetti
   - Ⓒ culture
   - Ⓓ mesquite

6. My grandfather used to play the _____ at weddings.
   - Ⓐ chile
   - Ⓑ accordion
   - Ⓒ confetti
   - Ⓓ barbecue

Comprehension

7. What is the goal of all the paintings that Carmen Lomas Garza paints?

Ⓐ to remember growing up in Kingsville, Texas

Ⓑ to encourage pride in the Mexican American heritage

Ⓒ to portray life in a Mexican family

Ⓓ to relive memories of growing up near the Mexican border

8. In the first painting, Garza portrays her brother and herself playing. Why is she standing on her toes?

Ⓐ She wants to get a better view of the horned toad.

Ⓑ She wants to see what's on the end of the stick.

Ⓒ She doesn't want to get bitten by fire ants.

Ⓓ She has holes in her shoes, and the ground is very hot.

9. Why does Carmen's grandfather shave off thorns from the *nopalitos*?

Ⓐ he needs them for another dish he will make

Ⓑ he doesn't have anything else to do

Ⓒ he is trying to sharpen his knife

Ⓓ they would hurt your mouth if you ate them

10. Why are *nopalitos* called "the food of last resort"?

Ⓐ They are available only at vacation resorts.

Ⓑ People eat them when the winter food supply runs out.

Ⓒ They taste so bad.

Ⓓ Mothers fix them when they can't think of anything else to cook.

11. In the painting showing the making of *empanadas*, why are all the family members standing?

Ⓐ The furniture is covered with *empanadas*.

Ⓑ The family must stand in order to make the *empanadas* correctly.

Ⓒ The family is getting ready to dance.

Ⓓ The chairs have been moved outside for a party.

© Harcourt

Practice Book
Lead the Way

12. Which statement is true about the Birthday Barbecue painting?

(A) There are not many people in the picture.

(B) Everyone is dancing.

(C) Many dogs are playing in the yard.

(D) Carmen has a big family.

13. The artist compares a night at El Jardín to heaven for all the following reasons **except** the _____ .

(A) music

(B) family members dancing together

(C) fireworks

(D) beautiful clothes

14. What do all the paintings in this selection have in common?

(A) They show unhappy events in the painter's life.

(B) They show children and adults together.

(C) They show celebrations of special events.

(D) They show special events from the painter's life.

15. What can the viewer determine from looking at the artist's paintings?

(A) that everyone is rich

(B) that it gets very hot in Texas

(C) that her family is too big

(D) that closeness within a family is important

16. How did the artist teach herself to draw?

(A) by practicing every day

(B) by watching other artists

(C) by painting Easter eggs

(D) by observing family celebrations

17. Why does the artist find it difficult at times to let her paintings be sold?

　Ⓐ She is used to having them around.

　Ⓑ They remind her of happy family events.

　Ⓒ She likes the way they are displayed.

　Ⓓ She has a strong affection for them.

18. The artist's paintings mostly show _____ .

　Ⓐ new clothing styles　　　Ⓑ outdoor scenes

　Ⓒ Mexican American culture　Ⓓ rooms in her house

19. How is decorating *cascarones* the same as coloring eggs? How is it different from coloring eggs?

_____

_____

_____

_____

_____

20. According to Garza, what are two reasons why being an artist can be difficult?

_____

_____

_____

_____

_____

Fly Traps! Plants That Bite Back

Directions: For items 1–18, fill in the circle in front of the correct answer. For items 19–20, write the answer.

Vocabulary

1. The butterwort eats insects, so it is a _____ plant.
- Ⓐ fertilizer
- Ⓑ dissolve
- Ⓒ boggiest
- Ⓓ carnivorous

2. My cake tasted bad because I _____ mixed in salt instead of sugar.
- Ⓐ chemicals
- Ⓑ accidentally
- Ⓒ dissolve
- Ⓓ victim

3. The spider will catch a _____ in its web.
- Ⓐ victim
- Ⓑ boggiest
- Ⓒ carnivorous
- Ⓓ chemicals

4. Our lawn is green and beautiful because Dad put _____ on it last week.
- Ⓐ accidentally
- Ⓑ victim
- Ⓒ fertilizer
- Ⓓ dissolve

5. The guide told us to stay out of the _____ area of the swamp because our feet would get wet.
- Ⓐ carnivorous
- Ⓑ boggiest
- Ⓒ chemicals
- Ⓓ victim

6. It is important to always handle _____ with great care because they can be dangerous.
- Ⓐ dissolve
- Ⓑ chemicals
- Ⓒ accidentally
- Ⓓ carnivorous

© Harcourt

7. Some chemicals will _____ in water, but others will not.

(A) dissolve   (B) fertilizer

(C) victim   (D) accidentally

Comprehension

8. Tangled stems with hundreds of tiny bubbles on them describes the _____ .

(A) sundew   (B) Venus flytrap

(C) bladderwort   (D) pitcher plant

9. To dissolve the bugs it traps, a bladderwort oozes _____ .

(A) water   (B) chemicals

(C) honey   (D) saliva

10. The bladderwort and the sundew are both carnivorous plants. They are different because _____ .

(A) the bladderwort grows on land and the sundew in water

(B) the bladderwort grows in water and the sundew on land

(C) there are over 200 different varieties of bladderworts and two varieties of sundews

(D) both plants have large trap doors from which a bug can escape

11. When a bug gets stuck on a sundew, the leaf _____ .

(A) snaps shut

(B) releases chemicals to dissolve it

(C) curls around it

(D) fries it in the sunlight

12. Why do little bugs stick to butterworts?

Ⓐ The plants have flat leaves like flypaper.

Ⓑ The bugs drown in a liquid.

Ⓒ The leaves snap shut.

Ⓓ The bugs are crushed.

13. What is harmful to plants that catch animals?

Ⓐ honey   Ⓑ tap water

Ⓒ fertilizer   Ⓓ rainwater

14. Which plant catches bugs with its trigger hairs and spiky rim?

Ⓐ the sundew

Ⓑ the pitcher plant

Ⓒ the cobra lily

Ⓓ the Venus flytrap

15. Why can small insects escape from the Venus flytrap?

Ⓐ They are more slippery.

Ⓑ They struggle harder.

Ⓒ They're too big to dissolve.

Ⓓ They're not worth eating.

16. Why are Venus flytraps rare today?

Ⓐ They only grow in a small section of the United States.

Ⓑ The swamps where they grow have been drained and cities built there.

Ⓒ People tried to make them grow bigger by fertilizing them and it killed them off.

Ⓓ Big insects have eaten all the leaves in trying to free their young from the traps.

© Harcourt

17. How does an insect become bug soup for the cobra lily?

    (A) The leaves of the cobra lily are like funnels with a sticky rim.

    (B) An insect falls into a pool at the bottom of a cobra lily leaf and can't climb out.

    (C) The leaves of the cobra lily are 18 inches long.

    (D) The cobra lily grows in ponds and looks like a cobra.

18. How do pitcher plants catch insects?

    (A) Their leaves have slippery sides with liquid at the bottom.

    (B) Insects stick to the rim of the pitcher plant.

    (C) The leaves are sensitive and snap shut on contact.

    (D) Just touching a pitcher plant leaf poisons an insect.

19. Why did pitcher plants probably get that name?

_____

_____

_____

_____

20. What can live inside a pitcher plant? Why?

_____

_____

_____

_____

The Down and Up Fall

Directions: For items 1–18, fill in the circle in front of the correct answer. For items 19–20, write the answer.

Vocabulary

1. We _____ our cafeteria into a beautiful garden by using flowers and foil to decorate.
   Ⓐ investigate
   Ⓑ transformed
   Ⓒ corridor
   Ⓓ apparently

2. Who can we ask to _____ the mystery for us?
   Ⓐ investigate
   Ⓑ enthusiastically
   Ⓒ decor
   Ⓓ corridor

3. We tried not to make noise as we tiptoed along the long _____ .
   Ⓐ decor
   Ⓑ apparently
   Ⓒ transformed
   Ⓓ corridor

4. That is the mother wolf, and these _____ are her pups.
   Ⓐ enthusiastically
   Ⓑ apparently
   Ⓒ investigate
   Ⓓ transformed

5. The choir sang the school song loudly and _____ .
   Ⓐ enthusiastically
   Ⓑ decor
   Ⓒ corridor
   Ⓓ investigate

6. The _____ in the old castle was elegant and fit with the style of the mansion.
   Ⓐ decor
   Ⓑ transformed
   Ⓒ apparently
   Ⓓ investigate

© Harcourt

Comprehension

7. This selection is most like realistic fiction for all of the following reasons **except** that the story _____ .

Ⓐ setting could be in a real place

Ⓑ took place a long time ago

Ⓒ characters are like those in real life

Ⓓ event could really happen

8. Why does Bolivia want to take Lucette to the rain forest?

Ⓐ The parrot will feel at home there.

Ⓑ Lucette wants to go there.

Ⓒ It sounds like fun.

Ⓓ She wants to show off the parrot.

9. For parrots and snakes, a tropical rain forest _____ .

Ⓐ is a hard place in which to live

Ⓑ is a natural habitat

Ⓒ has a climate that may kill them

Ⓓ is an unusual place in which to live

10. What does Bolivia worry will happen if she brings Lucette to school?

Ⓐ that Dr. Osborne will be afraid of the parrot

Ⓑ that it will be too warm and humid for Lucette

Ⓒ that Mr. Peters will tell her to take the parrot home

Ⓓ that it might be too stressful for Lucette

11. Why does Uncle Lou deliver Lucette to the school in the afternoon?

Ⓐ He has to take pictures of the rain forest for the newspaper.

Ⓑ Lucette is a nervous parrot.

Ⓒ Bolivia doesn't want the bird at school all day.

Ⓓ It is very noisy there.

12. How are tropical rain forests and botanical gardens alike?

    Ⓐ They both have visitors.

    Ⓑ Tropical plants grow there.

    Ⓒ They are in South America.

    Ⓓ They have snakes and birds.

13. Lucette probably says "Happy New Year" because she _____ .

    Ⓐ is afraid of people

    Ⓑ hears Dr. Osborne scream

    Ⓒ feels at home in the rain forest

    Ⓓ thinks that she's at a party

14. To create a simulation of a rain forest, the members of the nature club do all the following **except** _____ .

    Ⓐ turn on the sprinkler system

    Ⓑ bring animals

    Ⓒ use an electric heater and humidifier

    Ⓓ paint trees and plants

15. What causes the unexpected shower in the rain forest?

    Ⓐ the humidifier

    Ⓑ the heat setting off the sprinklers

    Ⓒ too much humidity and closed windows

    Ⓓ a hole in the ceiling

16. Kenny named his snakes after two famous _____ .

    Ⓐ astronauts

    Ⓑ teachers

    Ⓒ presidents

    Ⓓ scientists

17. Who shows a calm nature by responding to the sprinkler event by saying "This is how we keep education alive and exciting"?

(A) Mr. Golding

(B) Mr. Peters

(C) Dr. Osborne

(D) the custodian

18. Why does Dr. Osborne say she will never forget the afternoon or the snakes?

(A) She doesn't like snakes or getting wet.

(B) She doesn't like the idea of a rain forest in school.

(C) She is annoyed that students brought dirt into the school.

(D) She thinks that having the snakes and Lucette there is silly.

19. How do you know that the assistant principal was happy about the science project?

_____

_____

_____

_____

20. Do you think Mr. Peters and the science class will do another project? Why or why not?

_____

_____

_____

_____

Practice Book
Lead the Way